Means without End

Edited by

Sandra Buckley

Michael Hardt

Brian Massumi

THEORY OUT OF BOUNDS

Means without End

Notes on Politics

Giorgio Agamben

Translated by Vincenzo Binetti and Cesare Casarino

Theory out of Bounds   *Volume 20*

University of Minnesota Press

Minneapolis • London

Published by the University of Minnesota Press
111 Third Avenue South, Suite 290
Minneapolis, MN 55401-2520
http://www.upress.umn.edu

Printed in the United States of America on acid-free paper

LIBRARY OF CONGRESS CATALOGING-IN-PUBLICATION DATA
Agamben, Giorgio, 1942–
[Mezzi senza fine. English]
Means without end : notes on politics / Giorgio Agamben ;
translated by Vincenzo Binetti and Cesare Casarino.
p.   cm. — [Theory out of bounds ; v. 20]
Includes bibliographical references and index.

ISBN 978-0-8166-3035-6 (hc: alk. paper) — ISBN 978-0-8166-3036-3 (pb: alk. paper)

1. Political science — Philosophy.   I. Title.   II. Series.
JA71.J37 2000
320'.01 — dc21
00-008712

The University of Minnesota is an equal-opportunity educator and employer.

20 19 18 17 16 15 14   10 9 8 7 6

Contents

Preface

EACH OF the texts included in this volume attempts in its own way to think specific political problems. If politics today seems to be going through a protracted eclipse and appears in a subaltern position with respect to religion, economics, and even the law, that is so because, to the extent to which it has been losing sight of its own ontological status, it has failed to confront the transformations that gradually have emptied out its categories and concepts. Thus, in the following pages, genuinely political paradigms are sought in experiences and phenomena that usually are not considered political or that are considered only marginally so: the natural life of human beings (that zoē that was once excluded from properly political spheres and that, according to Foucault's analysis of biopolitics, has now been restored to the center of the polis); the state of exception (that temporary suspension of the rule of law that is revealed instead to constitute the fundamental structure of the legal system itself); the concentration camp (a zone of indifference between public and private as well as the hidden matrix of the political space in which we live); the refugee, formerly regarded as a marginal figure, who has become now the decisive factor of the modern nation-state by breaking the nexus between human being and citizen; language, whose hypertrophy and expropriation define the politics of the spectacular-democratic societies in which we live; and the sphere of gestures or pure means (that is, the sphere of those means that emancipate themselves from their relation to an end while still remaining means) posited as the proper sphere of politics.

All these texts refer, in various ways and according to the circumstances in which they were born, to investigations that are still open. At times they anticipate the original nuclei of those investigations and at others they present fragments and shards. (The first product of such investigations is the book titled *Homo Sacer.*) As such, these texts are destined to find their true sense only within the perspective of the completed work, that is, only within a rethinking of all the categories of our political tradition in light of the relation between sovereign power and naked life.[1]

PART I

Form-of-Life

THE ANCIENT Greeks did not have only one term to express what we mean by the word *life*. They used two semantically and morphologically distinct terms: *zoē*, which expressed the simple fact of living common to all living beings (animals, humans, or gods), and *bios*, which signified the form or manner of living peculiar to a single individual or group. In modern languages this opposition has gradually disappeared from the lexicon (and where it is retained, as in *biology* and *zoology*, it no longer indicates any substantial difference); one term only — the opacity of which increases in proportion to the sacralization of its referent — designates that naked presupposed common element that it is always possible to isolate in each of the numerous forms of life.

By the term *form-of-life*, on the other hand, I mean a life that can never be separated from its form, a life in which it is never possible to isolate something such as naked life.

A life that cannot be separated from its form is a life for which what is at stake in its way of living is living itself. What does this formulation mean? It defines a life — human life — in which the single ways, acts, and processes of living are never simply *facts* but always and above all *possibilities* of life, always and above all power.[1] Each behavior and each form of human living is never prescribed by a specific biological vocation, nor is it assigned by whatever necessity; instead, no matter how customary, repeated, and socially compulsory, it always retains the character of a possibility; that is, it always puts at stake living itself. That is why human beings — as beings of power who can do or not do, succeed or fail, lose themselves or find themselves — are the only beings for whom happiness is always at stake in their living, the only beings whose life is irremediably and painfully assigned to happiness. But this immediately constitutes the form-of-life as political life. "Civitatem . . . communitatem esse institutam propter vivere et bene vivere hominum in ea" [The state is a community instituted for the sake of the living and the well living of men in it].[2]

Political power as we know it, on the other hand, always founds itself — in the last instance — on the separation of a sphere of naked life from the context of the forms of life. In Roman law, *vita* [life] is not a juridical concept, but rather indicates the simple fact of living or a particular way of life. There is only one case in which the term *life* acquires a juridical meaning that transforms it into a veritable *terminus technicus*, and that is in the expression *vitae necisque potestas*, which designates the *pater*'s power of life and death over the male son. Yan Thomas has shown that, in this formula, *que* does not have disjunctive function and *vita* is nothing but a corollary of *nex*, the power to kill.[3]

Thus, life originally appears in law only as the counterpart of a power that threatens death. But what is valid for the *pater*'s right of life and death is even more valid for sovereign power (imperium), of which the former constitutes the originary cell. Thus, in the Hobbesian foundation of sovereignty, life in the state of nature is defined only by its being unconditionally exposed to a death threat (the limitless right of everybody over everything) and political life—that is, the life that unfolds under the protection of the Leviathan—is nothing but this very same life always exposed to a threat that now rests exclusively in the hands of the sovereign. The *puissance absolue et perpétuelle*, which defines state power, is not founded—in the last instance—on a political will but rather on naked life, which is kept safe and protected only to the degree to which it submits itself to the sovereign's (or the law's) right of life and death. (This is precisely the originary meaning of the adjective *sacer* [sacred] when used to refer to human life.) The state of exception, which is what the sovereign each and every time decides, takes place precisely when naked life—which normally appears rejoined to the multifarious forms of social life—is explicitly put into question and revoked as the ultimate foundation of political power. The ultimate subject that needs to be at once turned into the exception and included in the city is always naked life.

"The tradition of the oppressed teaches us that the 'state of emergency' in which we live is not the exception but the rule. We must attain to a conception of history that is in keeping with this insight."[4] Walter Benjamin's diagnosis, which by now is more than fifty years old, has lost none of its relevance. And that is so not really or not only because power no longer has today any form of legitimization other than emergency, and because power everywhere and continuously refers and appeals to emergency as well as laboring secretly to produce it. (How could we not think that a system that can no longer function at all except on the basis of emergency would not also be interested in preserving such an emergency at any price?) This is the case also and above all because naked life, which was the hidden foundation of sovereignty, has meanwhile become the dominant form of life everywhere. Life—in its state of exception that has now become the norm—is the naked life that in every context separates the forms of life from their cohering into a form-of-life. The Marxian scission between man and citizen is thus superseded by the division between naked life (ultimate and opaque bearer of sovereignty) and the multifarious forms of life abstractly recodified as social-juridical identities (the voter, the worker, the journalist, the student, but also the HIV-positive, the transvestite, the porno star, the elderly, the parent, the woman) that all rest on naked life. (To have mistaken such a naked life separate from its form, in its abjection, for a superior principle — sovereignty or the sacred — is the limit of Bataille's thought, which makes it useless to us.)

Foucault's thesis — according to which "what is at stake today is life" and hence politics has become biopolitics — is, in this sense, substantially correct. What is decisive, however, is the way in which one understands the sense of this transformation. What is left unquestioned in the contemporary debates on bioethics and biopolitics, in fact, is precisely what would deserve to be questioned before anything else, that is, the very biological concept of life. Paul Rabinow conceives of two models of life as symmetrical opposites: on the one hand, the experimental life[5] of the scientist who is ill with leukemia and who turns his very life into a laboratory for unlimited research and experimentation, and, on the other hand, the one who, in the name of life's sacredness, exasperates the antinomy between individual ethics and technoscience. Both models, however, participate without being aware of it in the same concept of naked life. This concept — which today presents itself under the guise of a scientific notion — is actually a secularized political concept. (From a strictly scientific point of view, the concept of life makes no sense. Peter and Jean Medawar tell us that, in biology, discussions about the real meaning of the words *life* and *death* are an index of a low level of conversation. Such words have no intrinsic meaning and such a meaning, therefore, cannot be clarified by deeper and more careful studies.)[6]

Such is the provenance of the (often unperceived and yet decisive) function of medical-scientific ideology within the system of power and the increasing use of pseudoscientific concepts for ends of political control. That same drawing of naked life that, in certain circumstances, the sovereign used to be able to exact from the forms of life is now massively and daily exacted by the pseudoscientific representations of the body, illness, and health, and by the "medicalization" of ever-widening spheres of life and of individual imagination.[7] Biological life, which is the secularized form of naked life and which shares its unutterability and impenetrability, thus constitutes the real forms of life literally as forms of *survival*: biological life remains inviolate in such forms as that obscure threat that can suddenly actualize itself in violence, in extraneousness, in illnesses, in accidents. It is the invisible sovereign that stares at us behind the dull-witted masks of the powerful who, whether or not they realize it, govern us in its name.

A political life, that is, a life directed toward the idea of happiness and cohesive with a form-of-life, is thinkable only starting from the emancipation from such a division, with the irrevocable exodus from any sovereignty. The question about the possibility of a nonstatist politics necessarily takes this form: Is today something like a form-of-life, a life for which living itself would be at stake in its own living, possible? Is today a *life of power* available?

I call *thought* the nexus that constitutes the forms of life in an inseparable context as form-of-life. I do not mean by this the individual exercise of an organ or of a psychic faculty, but rather an experience, an *experimentum* that has as its object the potential character of life and of human intelligence. To think does not mean merely to be affected by this or that thing, by this or that content of enacted thought, but rather at once to be affected by one's own receptiveness and experience in each and every thing that is thought a pure power of thinking. ("When thought has become each thing in the way in which a man who actually knows is said to do so ... its condition is still one of potentiality ... and thought is then able to think of itself.")[8]

Only if I am not always already and solely enacted, but rather delivered to a possibility and a power, only if living and intending and apprehending themselves are at stake each time in what I live and intend and apprehend—only if, in other words, there is thought—only then can a form of life become, in its own factness and thingness, *form-of-life*, in which it is never possible to isolate something like naked life.

The experience of thought that is here in question is always experience of a common power. Community and power identify one with the other without residues because the inherence of a communitarian principle to any power is a function of the necessarily potential character of any community. Among beings who would always already be enacted, who would always already be this or that thing, this or that identity, and who would have entirely exhausted their power in these things and identities—among such beings there could not be any community but only coincidences and factual partitions. We can communicate with others only through what in us—as much as in others—has remained potential, and any communication (as Benjamin perceives for language) is first of all communication not of something in common but of communicability itself. After all, if there existed one and only one being, it would be absolutely impotent. (That is why theologians affirm that God created the world ex nihilo, in other words, absolutely without power.) And there where I am capable, we are always already many (just as when, if there is a language, that is, a power of speech, there cannot then be one and only one being who speaks it.)

That is why modern political philosophy does not begin with classical thought, which had made of contemplation, of the *bios theoreticos*, a separate and solitary activity ("exile of the alone to the alone"), but rather only with Averroism, that is, with the thought of the one and only possible intellect common to all human beings, and, crucially, with Dante's affirmation—in *De Monarchia*—of the inherence of a multitude to the very power of thought:

It is clear that man's basic capacity is to have a potentiality or power for being intellectual. And since this
power cannot be completely actualized in a single
man or in any of the particular communities of men
above mentioned, there must be a multitude in mankind through whom this whole power can be actualized.... [T]he proper work of mankind taken as a
whole is to exercise continually its entire capacity for
intellectual growth, first, in theoretical matters, and,
secondarily, as an extension of theory, in practice.[9]

The diffuse intellectuality I am talking about and the
Marxian notion of a "general intellect"[10] acquire their
meaning only within the perspective of this experience.
They name the *multitudo* that inheres to the power of
thought as such. Intellectuality and thought are not a
form of life among others in which life and social production articulate themselves, but they are rather *the
unitary power that constitutes the multiple forms of life as
form-of-life*. In the face of state sovereignty, which can
affirm itself only by separating in every context naked
life from its form, they are the power that incessantly
reunites life to its form or prevents it from being disso-
ciated from its form. The act of distinguishing between
the mere, massive inscription of social knowledge into
the productive processes (an inscription that characterizes the contemporary phase of capitalism, the society
of the spectacle) and intellectuality as antagonistic power
and form-of-life — such an act passes through the experience of this cohesion and this inseparability. Thought
is form-of-life, life that cannot be segregated from its

form; and anywhere the intimacy of this inseparable life appears, in the materiality of corporeal processes and of habitual ways of life no less than in theory, there and only there is there thought. And it is this thought, this form-of-life, that, abandoning naked life to "Man" and to the "Citizen," who clothe it temporarily and represent it with their "rights," must become the guiding concept and the unitary center of the coming politics.

(1993)

Beyond Human Rights

IN 1943, Hannah Arendt published an article titled "We Refugees" in a small English-language Jewish publication, the *Menorah Journal*. At the end of this brief but significant piece of writing, after having polemically sketched the portrait of Mr. Cohn, the assimilated Jew who, after having been 150 percent German, 150 percent Viennese, 150 percent French, must bitterly realize in the end that "on ne parvient pas deux fois," she turns the condition of countryless refugee — a condition she herself was living — upside down in order to present it as the paradigm of a new historical consciousness. The refugees who have lost all rights and who, however, no longer want to be assimilated at all costs in a new national identity, but want instead to contemplate lucidly their condition, receive in exchange for assured unpopularity a priceless advantage: "History is no longer a closed book to them and politics is no longer the privilege of Gentiles. They know that the outlawing of the Jewish people of Europe has been followed closely by the outlawing of most European nations. Refugees driven from country to country represent the vanguard of their peoples."[1]

One ought to reflect on the meaning of this analysis, which after fifty years has lost none of its relevance. It is not only the case that the problem presents itself inside and outside of Europe with just as much urgency as then. It is also the case that, given the by now unstoppable decline of the nation-state and the general corrosion of traditional political-juridical categories, the refugee is perhaps the only thinkable figure for the people of our time and the only category in which one may see today—at least until the process of dissolution of the nation-state and of its sovereignty has achieved full completion—the forms and limits of a coming political community. It is even possible that, if we want to be equal to the absolutely new tasks ahead, we will have to abandon decidedly, without reservation, the fundamental concepts through which we have so far represented the subjects of the political (Man, the Citizen and its rights, but also the sovereign people, the worker, and so forth) and build our political philosophy anew starting from the one and only figure of the refugee.

The first appearance of refugees as a mass phenomenon took place at the end of World War I, when the fall of the Russian, Austro-Hungarian, and Ottoman empires, along with the new order created by the peace treaties, upset profoundly the demographic and territorial constitution of Central Eastern Europe. In a short period, 1.5 million White Russians, seven hundred thousand Armenians, five hundred thousand Bulgarians, a million Greeks, and hundreds of thousands of Germans, Hungarians, and Romanians left their countries. To these moving masses, one needs to add the explosive situation determined by the fact that about 30 percent of the population in the new states created by the peace treaties on the model of the nation-state (Yugoslavia and Czechoslovakia, for example), was constituted by minorities that had to be safeguarded by a series of international treaties—the so-called Minority Treaties—which very often were not enforced. A few years later, the racial laws in Germany and the civil war in Spain dispersed throughout Europe a new and important contingent of refugees.

We are used to distinguishing between refugees and stateless people, but this distinction was not then as simple as it may seem at first glance, nor is it even today. From the beginning, many refugees, who were not technically stateless, preferred to become such rather than return to their country. (This was the case with the Polish and Romanian Jews who were in France or Germany at the end of the war, and today it is the case with those who are politically persecuted or for whom returning to their countries would mean putting their own survival at risk.) On the other hand, Russian, Armenian, and Hungarian refugees were promptly denationalized by the new Turkish and Soviet governments. It is important to note how, starting with World War I, non (as was the case between the two world wars and is now once again), these organizations as well as the single states — all the solemn evocations of the inalienable rights of human beings notwithstanding — have proved to be absolutely incapable not only of solving the problem but also of facing it in an adequate manner. The whole question, therefore, was handed over to humanitarian organizations and to the police.

The reasons for such impotence lie not only in the selfishness and blindness of bureaucratic apparatuses, but also in the very ambiguity of the fundamental notions regulating the inscription of the *native* (that is, of life) in the juridical order of the nation-state. Hannah Arendt titled the chapter of her book *Imperialism* that concerns the refugee problem "The Decline of the Nation-State and the End of the Rights of Man."[2] One should try to take seriously this formulation, which indissolubly links the fate of the Rights of Man with the fate of the modern nation-state in such a way that the waning of the latter necessarily implies the obsolescence of the former. Here the paradox is that precisely the figure that should have embodied human rights more than any other — namely, the refugee — marked instead the radical crisis of the concept. The conception of human rights based on the supposed existence of a human being as such, Arendt tells us, proves to be untenable as soon as those who profess it find themselves confronted for the first time with people who have really lost every quality and every specific relation except for the pure fact of being human.[3] In the system of the nation-state, so-called sacred and inalienable human rights are revealed to be without any protection precisely when it is no longer possible to conceive of them as rights of the citizens of a state. This is implicit, after all, in the ambiguity of the very title of the 1789 *Déclaration des droits de l'homme et du citoyen,* in which it is unclear whether the two terms are to name two distinct realities or whether they are to form, instead, a hendiadys in which the first term is actually always already contained in the second.

That there is no autonomous space in the political order of the nation-state for something like the pure human in itself is evident at the very least from the fact that, even in the best of cases, the status of refugee has always been considered a temporary condition that ought to lead either to naturalization or to repatriation. A stable statute for the human in itself is inconceivable in the law of the nation-state.

It is time to cease to look at all the declarations of rights from 1789 to the present day as proclamations of eternal metajuridical values aimed at binding the legislator to the respect of such values; it is time, rather, to understand them according to their real function in the modern state. Human rights, in fact, represent first of all the originary figure for the inscription of natural naked life in the political-juridical order of the nation-state. Naked life (the human being), which in antiquity belonged to God and in the classical world was clearly distinct (as *zoē*) from political life (*bios*), comes to the forefront in the management of the state and becomes, so to speak, its earthly foundation. Nation-state means a state that makes nativity or birth [*nascita*] (that is, naked human life) the foundation of its own sovereignty. This is the meaning (and it is not even a hidden one) of the first three articles of the 1789 Declaration: it is only because this declaration inscribed (in articles 1 and 2) the native element in the heart of any political organization that it can firmly bind (in article 3) the principle of sovereignty to the nation (in conformity with its etymon, *native* [natío] originally meant simply "birth" [*nascita*]). The fiction that is implicit here is that *birth* [*nascita*] comes into being immediately as *nation*, so that there may not be any difference between the two moments. Rights, in other words, are attributed to the human being only to the degree to which he or she is the immediately vanishing presupposition (and, in fact, the presupposition that must never come to light as such) of the citizen.

If the refugee represents such a disquieting element in the order of the nation-state, this is so primarily because, by breaking the identity between the human and the citizen and that between nativity and nationality, it brings the originary fiction of sovereignty to crisis. Single exceptions to such a principle, of course, have always existed. What is new in our time is that growing sections of humankind are no longer representable inside the nation-state — and this novelty threatens the very foundations of the latter. Inasmuch as the refugee, an apparently marginal figure, unhinges the old trinity of state–nation–territory, it deserves instead to be regarded as the central figure of our political history. We should not forget that the first camps were built in Europe as spaces for controlling refugees, and that the succession of internment camps–concentration camps–extermination camps represents a perfectly real filiation. One of the few rules the Nazis constantly obeyed throughout the course of the "final solution" was that Jews and Gypsies could be sent to extermination camps only after having been fully denationalized (that is, after they had been stripped of even that second-class citizenship to which they had been relegated after the Nuremberg Laws). When their rights are no longer the rights of the citizen, that is when human beings are truly *sacred*, in the sense that this term used to have in the Roman law of the archaic period: doomed to death.

The concept of refugee must be resolutely separated from the concept of the "human rights," and the right of asylum (which in any case is by now in the process of being drastically restricted in the legislation of the European states) must no longer be considered as the conceptual category in which to inscribe the phenomenon of refugees. (One needs only to look at Agnes Heller's recent *Theses on the Right of Asylum* to realize that this cannot but lead today to awkward confusions.) The refugee should be considered for what it is, namely, nothing less than a limit-concept that at once brings a radical crisis to the principles of the nation-state and clears the way for a renewal of categories that can no longer be delayed.

Meanwhile, in fact, the phenomenon of so-called illegal immigration into the countries of the European Union has reached (and shall increasingly reach in the coming years, given the estimated twenty million immigrants from Central European countries) characteristics and proportions such that this reversal of perspective is fully justified. What industrialized countries face today is a permanently resident mass of noncitizens who do not want to be and cannot be either naturalized or repatriated. These noncitizens often have nationalities of origin, but, inasmuch as they prefer not to benefit from their own states' protection, they find themselves, as refugees, in a condition of de facto statelessness. Tomas Hammar has created the neologism of "denizens" for these noncitizen residents, a neologism that has the merit of showing how the concept of "citizen" is no longer adequate for describing the social-political reality of modern states.[4] On the other hand, the citizens of advanced industrial states (in the United States as well as Europe) demonstrate, through an increasing desertion of the codified instances of political participation, an evident propensity to turn into denizens, into noncitizen permanent residents, so that citizens and denizens — at least in certain social strata — are entering an area of potential indistinction. In a parallel way, xenophobic reactions and defensive mobilizations are on the rise, in conformity with the well-known principle according to which substantial assimilation in the presence of formal differences exacerbates hatred and intolerance.

Before extermination camps are reopened in Europe (something that is already starting to happen), it is necessary that the nation-states find the courage to question the very principle of the inscription of nativity as well as the trinity of state–nation–territory that is founded on that principle. It is not easy to indicate right now the ways in which all this may concretely happen. One of the options taken into consideration for solving the problem of Jerusalem is that it become — simultaneously and without any territorial partition — the capital of two different states. The paradoxical condition of reciprocal extraterritoriality (or, better yet, aterritoriality) that would thus be implied could be generalized as a model of new international relations. Instead of two national states separated by uncertain and threatening boundaries, it might be possible to imagine two political communities insisting on the same region and in a condition of exodus from each other — communities that would articulate each other via a series of reciprocal extraterritorialities in which the guiding concept would no longer be the *ius* (right) of the citizen but rather the *refugium* (refuge) of the singular. In an analogous way, we could conceive of Europe not as an impossible "Europe of the nations," whose catastrophe one can already foresee in the short run, but rather as an aterritorial or extraterritorial space in which all the (citizen and noncitizen) residents of the

European states would be in a position of exodus or refuge; the status of European would then mean the being-in-exodus of the citizen (a condition that obviously could also be one of immobility). European space would thus mark an irreducible difference between birth [*nascita*] and nation in which the old concept of people (which, as is well known, is always a minority) could again find a political meaning, thus decidedly opposing itself to the concept of nation (which has so far unduly usurped it).

This space would coincide neither with any of the homogeneous national territories nor with their *topographical* sum, but would rather act on them by articulating and perforating them *topologically* as in the Klein bottle or in the Möbius strip, where exterior and interior in-determine each other. In this new space, European cities would rediscover their ancient vocation of cities of the world by entering into a relation of reciprocal extraterritoriality.

As I write this essay, 425 Palestinians expelled by the state of Israel find themselves in a sort of no-man's-land. These men certainly constitute, according to Hannah Arendt's suggestion, "the vanguard of their people." But that is so not necessarily or not merely in the sense that they might form the originary nucleus of a future national state, or in the sense that they might solve the Palestinian question in a way just as insufficient as the way in which Israel has solved the Jewish question. Rather, the no-man's-land in which they are refugees has already started from this very moment to act back onto the territory of the state of Israel by perforating it

What Is a People?

ANY INTERPRETATION of the political meaning of the term *people* ought to start from the peculiar fact that in modern European languages this term always indicates also the poor, the underprivileged, and the excluded. The same term names the constitutive political subject as well as the class that is excluded — de facto, if not de jure — from politics.

The Italian term *popolo*, the French term *peuple*, and the Spanish term *pueblo* — along with the corresponding adjectives *popolare*, *populaire*, *popular* — and the late-Latin terms *populus* and *popularis* from which they all derive, designate in common parlance and in the political lexicon alike the whole of the citizenry as a unitary body politic (as in "the Italian people" or in "*giudice popolare*" [juryman]) as well as those who belong to inferior classes (as in *homme du peuple* [man of the people], *rione popolare* [working-class neighborhood], *front populaire* [popular front]). Even the English *people*—whose sense is more undifferentiated—does retain the meaning of *ordinary people* as opposed to the rich and the aristocracy. In the American Constitution one thus reads without any sort of distinction: "We, the people of the United States..."; but when Lincoln in the Gettysburg Address invokes a "government of the people, by the people, for the people," the repetition implicitly sets another people against the first. The extent to which such an ambiguity was essential even during the French Revolution (that is, at the very moment in which people's sovereignty was claimed as a principle) is witnessed by the decisive role played in it by a sense of compassion for the people intended as the excluded class. Hannah Arendt reminds us that:

> The very definition of the word was born out of compassion, and the term became the equivalent for misfortune and unhappiness—*le peuple, les malheureux m'applaudissent*, as Robespierre was wont to say; *le peuple toujours malheureux*, as even Sieyès, one of the least sentimental and most sober figures of the Revolution, would put it.[1]

But this is already a double concept for Jean Bodin—albeit in a different sense—in the chapter of *Les Six Livres de la République* in which he defines Democracy or *État Populaire*: while the *menu peuple* is that which it is wise to exclude from political power, the *peuple en corps* is intended as entitled to sovereignty.

Such a widespread and constant semantic ambiguity cannot be accidental: it surely reflects an ambiguity inherent in the nature and function of the concept of *people* in Western politics. It is as if, in other words, what we call people was actually not a unitary subject but rather a dialectical oscillation between two opposite poles: on the one hand, the *People* as a whole and as an integral body politic and, on the other hand, the *people* as a subset and as fragmentary multiplicity of needy and excluded bodies; on the one hand, an inclusive concept that pretends to be without remainder while, on the other hand, an exclusive concept known to afford no hope; at one pole, the total state of the sovereign and integrated citizens and, at the other pole, the banishment—either court of miracles or camp—of the wretched, the oppressed, and the vanquished. There exists no single and compact referent for the term *people* anywhere: like many fundamental political concepts (which, in this respect, are similar to Abel and Freud's *Urworte* or to Dumont's hierarchical relations), *people* is a polar concept that indicates a double movement and a complex relation between two extremes. This also means, however, that the constitution of the human species into a body politic comes into being through a fundamental split and that in the concept of *people* we can easily recognize the conceptual pair identified earlier as the defining category of the original

political structure: naked life (*people*) and political existence (*People*), exclusion and inclusion, *zoē* and *bios*. *The
concept of people always already contains within itself the fundamental biopolitical fracture. It is what cannot be included
in the whole of which it is a part as well as what cannot belong to the whole in which it is always already included.*

Hence the contradictions and aporias that
such a concept creates every time that it is invoked and
brought into play on the political stage. It is what always
already is, as well as what has yet to be realized; it is the
pure source of identity and yet it has to redefine and pu-
rify itself continuously according to exclusion, language,
blood, and territory. It is what has in its opposite pole
the very essence that it itself lacks; its realization therefore coincides with its own abolition; it must negate itself through its opposite in order to be. (Hence the specific aporias of the workers' movement that turns toward
the people and at the same time aims at its abolition.)
The concept of people—brandished each and every time
as the bloody flag of reaction and as the faltering banner of revolutions and popular fronts—always contains
a more original split than the one between enemy and
friend, an incessant civil war that at once divides this
concept more radically than any conflict and keeps it
united and constitutes it more firmly than any identity.
As a matter of fact, what Marx calls class struggle—which
occupies such a central place in his thought, even though
he never defines it substantially—is nothing other than
this internecine war that divides every people and that
shall come to an end only when *People* and *people* coin-

cide, in the classless society or in the messianic king-
dom, and only when there shall no longer be, properly
speaking, any people.

If this is the case—if the concept of *people* necessarily
contains within itself the fundamental biopolitical fracture—it is possible to read anew some decisive pages of
the history of our century. If the struggle between the
two peoples has always been in process, in fact, it has
undergone in our time one last and paroxysmal acceler-
ation. In ancient Rome, the split internal to the people
was juridically sanctioned by the clear distinction between *populus* and *plebs*—each with its own institutions
and magistrates—just as in the Middle Ages the division
between artisans [*popolo minuto*] and merchants [*popolo
grasso*] used to correspond to a precise articulation of different arts and crafts. But when, starting with the French
Revolution, sovereignty is entrusted solely to the people,
the *people* become an embarrassing presence, and poverty
and exclusion appear for the first time as an intolerable
scandal in every sense. In the modern age, poverty and
exclusion are not only economic and social concepts but
also eminently political categories. (The economism and
"socialism" that seem to dominate modern politics actually have a political, or, rather, a *biopolitical*, meaning.)
From this perspective, our time is nothing
other than the methodical and implacable attempt to
fill the split that divides the people by radically eliminating the people of the excluded. Such an attempt brings
together, according to different modalities and horizons,

both the right and the left, both capitalist countries and socialist countries, which have all been united in the plan to produce one single and undivided people — an ultimately futile plan that, however, has been partially realized in all industrialized countries. The obsession with development is so effective in our time because it coincides with the biopolitical plan to produce a people without fracture.

When seen in this light, the extermination of the Jews in Nazi Germany acquires a radically new meaning. As a people that refuses integration in the national body politic (it is assumed, in fact, that its assimilation is actually only a feigned one), the Jews are the representatives par excellence and almost the living symbol of the *people*, of that naked life that modernity necessarily creates within itself but whose presence it is no longer able to tolerate in any way. We ought to understand the lucid fury with which the German *Volk* — representative par excellence of the people as integral body politic — tried to eliminate the Jews forever as precisely the terminal phase of the internecine struggle that divides *People* and *people*. With the final solution — which included Gypsies and other unassimilable elements for a reason — Nazism tried obscurely and in vain to free the Western political stage from this intolerable shadow so as to produce finally the German *Volk* as the people that has been able to heal the original biopolitical fracture. (And that is why the Nazi chiefs repeated so obstinately that by eliminating Jews and Gypsies they were actually working also for the other European peoples.)

Paraphrasing the Freudian postulate on the relation between *Es* and *Ich*, one might say that modern biopolitics is supported by the principle according to which "where there is naked life, there has to be a *People*," as long as one adds immediately that this principle is valid also in its inverse formulation, which prescribes that "where there is a *People*, there shall be naked life." The fracture that was believed to have been healed by eliminating the *people* — namely, the Jews, who are its symbol — reproduced itself anew, thereby turning the whole German people into sacred life that is doomed to death and into a biological body that has to be infinitely purified (by eliminating the mentally ill and the carriers of hereditary diseases). And today, in a different and yet analogous way, the capitalistic-democratic plan to eliminate the poor not only reproduces inside itself the people of the excluded but also turns all the populations of the Third World into naked life. Only a politics that has been able to come to terms with the fundamental biopolitical split of the West will be able to arrest this oscillation and put an end to the civil war that divides the peoples and the cities of the Earth.

(1995)

What Is a Camp?

WHAT HAPPENED in the camps exceeds the juridical concept of crime to such an extent that the specific political-juridical structure within which those events took place has often been left simply unexamined. The camp is the place in which the most absolute *conditio inhumana* ever to appear on Earth was realized: this is ultimately all that counts for the victims as well as for posterity. Here I will deliberately set out in the opposite direction. Rather than deducing the definition of camp from the events that took place there, I will ask instead: *What is a camp? What is its political-juridical structure? How could such events have taken place there?* This will lead us to look at the camp not as a historical fact and an anomaly that—though admittedly still with us—belongs nonetheless to the past, but rather in some sense as the hidden matrix and *nomos* of the political space in which we still live.

Historians debate whether the first appearance of camps ought to be identified with the *campos de concentraciones* that were created in 1896 by the Spaniards in Cuba in order to repress the insurrection of that colony's population, or rather with the *concentration camps* into which the English herded the Boers at the beginning of the twentieth century. What matters here is that in both cases one is dealing with the extension to an entire civilian population of a state of exception linked to a colonial war. The camps, in other words, were not born out of ordinary law, and even less were they the product — as one might have believed — of a transformation and a development of prison law; rather, they were born out of the state of exception and martial law. This is even more evident in the case of the Nazi *Lager*, whose origin and juridical regime is well documented. It is well known that the juridical foundation of internment was not ordinary law but rather the *Schutzhaft* (literally, protective custody), which was a juridical institution of Prussian derivation that Nazi jurists sometimes considered a measure of preventive policing inasmuch as it enabled the "taking into custody" of individuals regardless of any relevant criminal behavior and exclusively in order to avoid threats to the security of the state. The origin of the *Schutzhaft*, however, resides in the Prussian law on the state of siege that was passed on June 4, 1851, and that was extended to the whole of Germany (with the exception of Bavaria) in 1871, as well as in the earlier Prussian law on the "protection of personal freedom"

(*Schutz der persönlichen Freiheit*) that was passed on Feb-
ruary 12, 1850. Both these laws were applied widely during World War I.

One cannot overestimate the importance of
this constitutive nexus between state of exception and
concentration camp for a correct understanding of the
nature of the camp. Ironically, the "protection" of freedom that is in question in the *Schutzhaft* is a protection
against the suspension of the law that characterizes the
state of emergency. What is new here is that this institution is dissolved by the state of exception on which it
was founded and is allowed to continue to be in force
under normal circumstances. *The camp is the space that
opens up when the state of exception starts to become the rule.*
In it, the state of exception, which was essentially a temporal suspension of the state of law, acquires a permanent spatial arrangement that, as such, remains constantly
outside the normal state of law. When Himmler decided,
in March 1933, on the occasion of the celebrations of
Hitler's election to the chancellorship of the Reich, to
create a "concentration camp for political prisoners" at
Dachau, this camp was immediately entrusted to the SS
and, thanks to the *Schutzhaft*, was placed outside the
jurisdiction of criminal law as well as prison law, with
which it neither then nor later ever had anything to
do. Dachau, as well as the other camps that were soon
added to it (Sachsenhausen, Buchenwald, Lichtenberg),
remained virtually always operative: the number of in-
mates varied and during certain periods (in particular, be-

tween 1935 and 1937, before the deportation of the Jews began) it decreased to 7,500 people; the camp as such, however, had become a permanent reality in Germany.

One ought to reflect on the paradoxical status of the camp as space of exception: the camp is a piece of territory that is placed outside the normal juridical order; for all that, however, it is not simply an external space. According to the etymological meaning of the term *exception* (*ex-capere*), what is being excluded in the camp is *captured outside*, that is, it is included by virtue of its very exclusion. Thus, what is being captured under the rule of law is first of all the very state of exception. In other words, if sovereign power is founded on the ability to decide on the state of exception, the camp is the structure in which the state of exception is permanently realized. Hannah Arendt observed once that what comes to light in the camps is the principle that supports totalitarian domination and that common sense stubbornly refuses to admit to, namely, the principle according to which anything is possible. It is only because the camps constitute a space of exception—a space in which the law is completely suspended—that everything is truly possible in them. If one does not understand this particular political-juridical structure of the camps, whose vocation is precisely to realize permanently the exception, the incredible events that took place in them remain entirely unintelligible. The people who entered the camp moved about in a zone of indistinction between the outside and the inside, the exception and the rule, the licit and the illicit, in which every juridical protection had disappeared; moreover, if they were Jews, they had already been deprived of citizenship rights by the Nuremberg Laws and were later completely denationalized at the moment of the "final solution." *Inasmuch as its inhabitants have been stripped of every political status and reduced completely to naked life, the camp is also the most absolute biopolitical space that has ever been realized — a space in which power confronts nothing other than pure biological life without any mediation.* The camp is the paradigm itself of political space at the point in which politics becomes biopolitics and the *homo sacer* becomes indistinguishable from the citizen. The correct question regarding the horrors committed in the camps, therefore, is not the question that asks hypocritically how it could have been possible to commit such atrocious horrors against other human beings; it would be more honest, and above all more useful, to investigate carefully how — that is, thanks to what juridical procedures and political devices — human beings could have been so completely deprived of their rights and prerogatives to the point that committing any act toward them would no longer appear as a crime (at this point, in fact, truly anything had become possible).

If this is the case, if the essence of the camp consists in the materialization of the state of exception and in the consequent creation of a space for naked life as such, we will then have to admit to be facing a camp virtually every time that such a structure is created, regardless of the nature of the crimes committed in it and regardless of the denomination and specific topography it might have. The soccer stadium in Bari in which the Italian police temporarily herded Albanian illegal immigrants in 1991 before sending them back to their country, the cycle-racing track in which the Vichy authorities rounded up the Jews before handing them over to the Germans, the refugee camp near the Spanish border where Antonio Machado died in 1939, as well as the *zones d'attente* in French international airports in which foreigners requesting refugee status are detained will all have to be considered camps. In all these cases, an apparently anodyne place (such as the Hotel Arcade near the Paris airport) delimits instead a space in which, for all intents and purposes, the normal rule of law is suspended and in which the fact that atrocities may or may not be committed does not depend on the law but rather on the civility and ethical sense of the police that act temporarily as sovereign. This is the case, for example, during the four days foreigners may be kept in the *zone d'attente* before the intervention of French judicial authorities. In this sense, even certain outskirts of the great postindustrial cities as well as the gated communities of the United States are beginning today to look like camps, in which naked life and political life, at least in determinate moments, enter a zone of absolute indeterminacy.

From this perspective, the birth of the camp in our time appears to be an event that marks in a decisive way the political space itself of modernity. This birth takes place when the political system of the modern nation-state—

founded on the functional nexus between a determinate localization (territory) and a determinate order (the state), which was mediated by automatic regulations for the inscription of life (birth or nation) — enters a period of permanent crisis and the state decides to undertake the management of the biological life of the nation directly as its own task. In other words, if the structure of the nation-state is defined by three elements — *territory, order,* and *birth* — the rupture of the old *nomos* does not take place in the two aspects that, according to Carl Schmitt, used to constitute it (that is, localization, *Ortung,* and order, *Ordnung*), but rather at the site in which naked life is inscribed in them (that is, there where inscription turns *birth* into *nation*). There is something that no longer functions in the traditional mechanisms that used to regulate this inscription, and the camp is the new hidden regulator of the inscription of life in the order — or, rather, it is the sign of the system's inability to function without transforming itself into a lethal machine. It is important to note that the camps appeared at the same time that the new laws on citizenship and on the denationalization of citizens were issued (not only the Nuremberg Laws on citizenship in the Reich but also the laws on the denationalization of citizens that were issued by almost all the European states, including France, between 1915 and 1933). The state of exception, which used to be essentially a temporary suspension of the order, becomes now a new and stable spatial arrangement inhabited by that naked life that increasingly cannot be inscribed into the order. *The increasingly widen-*

ing gap between birth (naked life) and nation-state is the new fact of the politics of our time and what we are calling "camp" is this disparity. To an order without localization (that is, the state of exception during which the law is suspended) corresponds now a localization without order (that is, the camp as permanent space of exception). The political system no longer orders forms of life and juridical norms in a determinate space; rather, it contains within itself a *dislocating localization* that exceeds it and in which virtually every form of life and every norm can be captured. The camp intended as a dislocating localization is the hidden matrix of the politics in which we still live, and we must learn to recognize it in all of its metamorphoses. The camp is the fourth and inseparable element that has been added to and has broken up the old trinity of nation (birth), state, and territory.

It is from this perspective that we need to see the reappearance of camps in a form that is, in a certain sense, even more extreme in the territories of the former Yugoslavia. What is happening there is not at all, as some interested observers rushed to declare, a redefinition of the old political system according to new ethnic and territorial arrangements, that is, a simple repetition of the processes that culminated in the constitution of the European nation-states. Rather, we note there an irreparable rupture of the old *nomos* as well as a dislocation of populations and human lives according to entirely new lines of flight. That is why the camps of ethnic rape are so crucially important. If the Nazis never thought of carrying out the "final solution" by impregnating Jewish

women, that is because the principle of birth, which en-
sured the inscription of life in the order of the nation-
state, was in some way still functioning, even though it
was profoundly transformed. This principle is now adrift:
it has entered a process of dislocation in which its functioning is becoming patently impossible and in which we
can expect not only new camps but also always new and
more delirious normative definitions of the inscription
of life in the city. The camp, which is now firmly settled
inside it, is the new biopolitical *nomos* of the planet.

(1994)

PART **II**

Notes on Gesture

1. By the end of the nineteenth century, the Western bourgeoisie had definitely lost its gestures.

IN 1886, Gilles de la Tourette, "ancien interne des Hôpitaux de Paris et de la Salpêtrière," published with Delahaye et Lecrosnier the *Études cliniques et physiologiques sur la marche* [Clinical and physiological studies on the gait]. It was the first time that one of the most common human gestures was analyzed with strictly scientific methods. Fifty-three years earlier, when the bourgeoisie's good conscience was still intact, the plan of a general pathology of social life announced by Balzac had produced nothing more than the fifty rather disappointing pages of the *Théorie de la démarche* [Theory of bearing]. Nothing is more revealing of the distance (not only a temporal one) separating the two attempts than the description

Gilles de la Tourette gives of a human step. Whereas Balzac saw only the expression of moral character, de la Tourette employed a gaze that is already a prophecy of what cinematography would later become:

> While the left leg acts as the fulcrum, the right foot is raised from the ground with a coiling motion that starts at the heel and reaches the tip of the toes, which leave the ground last; the whole leg is now brought forward and the foot touches the ground with the heel. At this very instant, the left foot—having ended its revolution and leaning only on the tip of the toes—leaves the ground; the left leg is brought forward, gets closer to and then passes the right leg, and the left foot touches the ground with the heel, while the right foot ends its own revolution.[1]

Only an eye gifted with such a vision could have perfected that footprint method of which Gilles de la Tourette was, with good reason, so proud. An approximately seven- or eight-meter-long and fifty-centimeter-wide roll of white wallpaper was nailed to the ground and then divided in half lengthwise by a pencil-drawn line. The soles of the experiment's subject were then smeared with iron sesquioxide powder, which stained them with a nice red rust color. The footprints that the patient left while walking along the dividing line allowed a perfect measurement of the gait according to various parameters (length of the step, lateral swerve, angle of inclination, etc.).

If we observe the footprint reproductions published by Gilles de la Tourette, it is impossible not to think about the series of snapshots that Muybridge was producing in those same years at the University of Pennsylvania using a battery of twenty-four photographic lenses. "Man walking at normal speed," "running man with shotgun," "walking woman picking up a jug," "walking woman sending a kiss": these are the happy and visible twins of the unknown and suffering creatures that had left those traces.

The *Étude sur une affection nerveuse caractérisée par de l'incoordination motrice accompagnée d'écholalie et de coprolalie* [Study on a nervous condition characterized by lack of motor coordination accompanied by echolalia and coprolalia] was published a year before the studies on the gait came out. This book defined the clinical profile of what later would be called Gilles de la Tourette syndrome. On this occasion, the same distancing that the footprint method had enabled in the case of a most common gesture was applied to the description of an amazing proliferation of tics, spasmodic jerks, and mannerisms — a proliferation that cannot be defined in any way other than as a generalized catastrophe of the sphere of gestures. Patients can neither start nor complete the simplest of gestures. If they are able to start a movement, this is interrupted and broken up by shocks lacking any coordination and by tremors that give the impression that the whole musculature is engaged in a dance (*chorea*) that is completely independent of any ambulatory end. The equivalent of this disorder in the sphere of the gait is exemplarily described by Jean-Martin Charcot in his famous *Leçons du mardi*:

He sets off—with his body bent forward and with his lower limbs rigidly and entirely adhering one to the other—by leaning on the tip of his toes. His feet then begin to slide on the ground somehow, and he proceeds through some sort of swift tremor.... When the patient hurls himself forward in such a way, it seems as if he might fall forward any minute; in any case, it is practically impossible for him to stop all by himself and often he needs to throw himself on an object nearby. He looks like an automaton that is being propelled by a spring: there is nothing in these rigid, jerky, and convulsive movements that resembles the nimbleness of the gait.... Finally, after several attempts, he sets off and—in conformity to the aforementioned mechanism—slides over the ground rather than walking: his legs are rigid, or, at least, they bend ever so slightly, while his steps are somehow substituted for as many abrupt tremors.[2]

What is most extraordinary is that these disorders, after having been observed in thousands of cases since 1885, practically cease to be recorded in the first years of the twentieth century, until the day when Oliver Sacks, in the winter of 1971, thought that he noticed three cases of Tourettism in the span of a few minutes while walking along the streets of New York City. One of the hypotheses that could be put forth in order to explain this disappearance is that in the meantime ataxia, tics, and dystonia had become the norm and that at some point everybody had lost control of their gestures and was walking and gesticulating frantically. This is the impression, at any rate, that one has when watching the films that Marey and Lumière began to shoot exactly in those years.

2. In the cinema, a society that has lost its gestures tries at once to reclaim what it has lost and to record its loss.

An age that has lost its gestures is, for this reason, obsessed by them. For human beings who have lost every sense of naturalness, each single gesture becomes a destiny. And the more gestures lose their ease under the action of invisible powers, the more life becomes indecipherable. In this phase the bourgeoisie, which just a few decades earlier was still firmly in possession of its symbols, succumbs to interiority and gives itself up to psychology.

  Nietzsche represents the specific moment in European culture when this polar tension between the obliteration and loss of gestures and their transfiguration into fate reaches its climax. The thought of the eternal return, in fact, is intelligible only as a gesture in which power and act, naturalness and manner, contingency and necessity become indiscernible (ultimately, in other words, only as theater). *Thus Spake Zarathustra* is the ballet of a humankind that has lost its gestures. And when the age realized this, it then began (but it was too late!) the precipitous attempt to recover the lost gestures in extremis. The dance of Isadora Duncan and Sergei Diaghilev, the novel of Proust, the great *Jugendstil* poetry from Pascoli to Rilke, and, finally and most exemplarily, the silent movie trace the magic circle in which humanity tried for the last time to evoke what was slipping through its fingers forever.

During the same years, Aby Warburg began those investigations that only the myopia of a psychologizing history of art could have defined as a "science of the image." The main focus of those investigations was, rather, the gesture intended as a crystal of historical memory, the process by which it stiffened and turned into a destiny, as well as the strenuous attempt of artists and philosophers (an attempt that, according to Warburg, was on the verge of insanity) to redeem the gesture from its destiny through a dynamic polarization. Because of the fact that this research was conducted through the medium of images, it was believed that the image was also its object. Warburg instead transformed the image into a decisively historical and dynamic element. (Likewise, the image will provide for Jung the model of the archetypes' metahistorical sphere.) In this sense, the atlas *Mnemosyne* that he left incomplete and that consists of almost a thousand photographs is not an immovable repertoire of images but rather a representation in virtual movement of Western humanity's gestures from classical Greece to Fascism (in other words, something that is closer to De Jorio than Panofsky). Inside each section, the single images should be considered more as film stills than as autonomous realities (at least in the same way in which Benjamin once compared the dialectical image to those little books, forerunners of cinematography, that gave the impression of movement when the pages were turned over rapidly).

3. The element of cinema is gesture and not image.

Gilles Deleuze has argued that cinema erases the fallacious psychological distinction between image as psychic reality and movement as physical reality. Cinematographic images are neither *poses éternelles* (such as the forms of the classical age) nor *coupes immobiles* of movement, but rather *coupes mobiles*, images themselves in movement, that Deleuze calls movement-images.[3]

It is necessary to extend Deleuze's argument and show how it relates to the status of the image in general within modernity. This implies, however, that the mythical rigidity of the image has been broken and that here, properly speaking, there are no images but only gestures. Every image, in fact, is animated by an antinomic polarity: on the one hand, images are the reification and obliteration of a gesture (it is the *imago* as death mask or as symbol); on the other hand, they preserve the *dynamis* intact (as in Muybridge's snapshots or in any sports photograph). The former corresponds to the recollection seized by voluntary memory, while the latter corresponds to the image flashing in the epiphany of involuntary memory. And while the former lives in magical isolation, the latter always refers beyond itself to a whole of which it is a part. Even the *Mona Lisa*, even *Las Meninas* could be seen not as immovable and eternal forms, but as fragments of a gesture or as stills of a lost film wherein only they would regain their true meaning. And that is so because a certain kind of *litigatio*, a paralyzing power whose spell we need to break, is continuously at work in every image; it is as if a silent invocation calling for the liberation of the image into gesture arose from the entire history of art. This is what in ancient Greece was expressed by the legends in which statues break the ties holding them and begin to move. But this is also the intention that philosophy entrusts to the idea, which is not at all an immobile archetype as common interpretations would have it, but rather a constellation in which phenomena arrange themselves in a gesture.

Cinema leads images back to the homeland of gesture. According to the beautiful definition implicit in Beckett's *Traum und Nacht*, it is the dream of a gesture. The duty of the director is to introduce into this dream the element of awakening.

4. Because cinema has its center in the gesture and not in the image, it belongs essentially to the realm of ethics and politics (and not simply to that of aesthetics).

What is a gesture? A remark of Varro contains a valuable indication. He inscribes the gesture into the sphere of action, but he clearly sets it apart from acting (*agere*) and from making (*facere*):

> The third stage of action is, they say, that in which they *faciunt* "make" something: in this, on account of the likeness among *agere* "to act" and *gerere* "to carry or carry on," a certain error is committed by those who think that it is only one thing. For a person can

facere something and not *agere* it, as a poet *facit* "makes" a play and does not act it, and on the other hand the actor *agit* "acts" it and does not make it, and so a play *fit* "is made" by the poet, not acted, and *agitur* "is acted" by the actor, not made. On the other hand, the general [*imperator*], in that he is said to *gerere* "carry on" affairs, in this neither *facit* "makes" nor *agit* "acts," but *gerit* "carries on," that is, supports, a meaning transferred from those who *gerunt* "carry" burdens, because they support them. (VI VIII 77)[4]

What characterizes gesture is that in it nothing is being produced or acted, but rather something is being endured and supported. The gesture, in other words, opens the sphere of *ethos* as the more proper sphere of that which is human. But in what way is an action endured and supported? In what way does a *res* become a *res gesta*, that is, in what way does a simple fact become an event? The Varronian distinction between *facere* and *agere* is derived, in the end, from Aristotle. In a famous passage of the *Nicomachean Ethics*, he opposes the two terms as follows: "For production [*poiesis*] has an end other than itself, but action [*praxis*] does not: good action is itself an end" (VI 1140b).[5] What is new in Varro is the identification of a third type of action alongside the other two: if producing is a means in view of an end and praxis is an end without means, the gesture then breaks with the false alternative between ends and means that paralyzes morality and presents instead means that, *as such*, evade the orbit of mediality without becoming, for this reason, ends.

Nothing is more misleading for an understanding of gesture, therefore, than representing, on the one hand, a sphere of means as addressing a goal (for example, marching seen as a means of moving the body from point A to point B) and, on the other hand, a separate and superior sphere of gesture as a movement that has its end in itself (for example, dance seen as an aesthetic dimension). Finality without means is just as alienating as mediality that has meaning only with respect to an end. If dance is gesture, it is so, rather, because it is nothing more than the endurance and the exhibition of the media character of corporal movements. *The gesture is the exhibition of a mediality: it is the process of making a means visible as such.* It allows the emergence of the being-in-a-medium of human beings and thus it opens the ethical dimension for them. But, just as in a pornographic film, people caught in the act of performing a gesture that is simply a means addressed to the end of giving pleasure to others (or to themselves) are kept suspended in and by their own mediality—for the only reason of being shot and exhibited in their mediality—and can become the medium of a new pleasure for the audience (a pleasure that would otherwise be incomprehensible); or, just as in the case of the mime, when gestures addressed to the most familiar ends are exhibited as such and are thus kept suspended "entre le désir et l'accomplissement, la perpétration et son souvenir" [between desire and fulfillment, perpetration and its recollection]—in what Mallarmé calls a *milieu pur*, so what is relayed to human beings in gestures is not the sphere of an end in itself but rather the sphere of a pure and endless mediality.

It is only in this way that the obscure Kantian expression "purposiveness without purpose" acquires a concrete meaning. Such a finality in the realm of means is that power of the gesture that interrupts the gesture in its very being-means and only in this way can exhibit it, thereby transforming a *res* into a *res gesta*. In the same way, if we understand the "word" as the means of communication, then to show a word does not mean to have at one's disposal a higher level (a metalanguage, itself incommunicable within the first level), starting from which we could make that word an object of communication; it means, rather, to expose the word in its own mediality, in its own being a means, without any transcendence. The gesture is, in this sense, communication of a communicability. It has precisely nothing to say because what it shows is the being-in-language of human beings as pure mediality. However, because being-in-language is not something that could be said in sentences, the gesture is essentially always a gesture of not being able to figure something out in language; it is always a *gag* in the proper meaning of the term, indicating first of all something that could be put in your mouth to hinder speech, as well as in the sense of the actor's improvisation meant to compensate a loss of memory or an inability to speak. From this point derives not only the proximity between gesture and philosophy, but also the one between philosophy and cinema. Cinema's essential "silence" (which has nothing to do with the presence or absence of a sound track) is, just like the silence of philosophy, exposure of the being-in-language of human beings: pure gesturality. The Wittgensteinian definition of the mystic as the appearing of what cannot be said is literally a definition of the *gag*. And every great philosophical text is the *gag* exhibiting language itself, being-in-language itself as a gigantic loss of memory, as an incurable speech defect.

5. *Politics is the sphere of pure means, that is, of the absolute and complete gesturality of human beings.*

(1992)

·

Languages and Peoples

BANDS OF Gypsies made their appearance in France during the first decades of the fifteenth century—a period characterized by wars and disorders. They said they came from Egypt and were led by individuals who called themselves dukes *in Egypto parvo* or counts *in Egypto minori*:

> The first groups of Gypsies were sighted on the territory of present-day France in 1419.... On August 22, 1419, they appear in the town of Châtillon-en-Dombe; the following day, the group reaches Saint Laurent de Mâcon—six leagues away—led by a certain Andrea, duke of Minor Egypt.... In July 1422, an even larger band goes down to Italy.... In August 1427, Gypsies appear for the first time at the doors of Paris, after having traveled through a war-torn France.... The capital is invaded by the English and

the entire Île-de-France is infested with bandits. Some groups of Gypsies, led by dukes or counts *in Egypto parvo* or *in Egypto minori,* cross the Pyrenees and go as far as Barcelona.[1]

Historians date the birth of *argot,* the secret language of the *coquillards* and other gangs of evildoers, roughly to this same period. These gangs prospered in the tormented years that marked the shift from medieval society to the modern state: "It is true, as he says, that the above mentioned *coquillards* use among themselves a secret language [*langage exquis*] that others cannot comprehend if it is not taught to them. Furthermore, through this language they can recognize the members of the so-called *Coquille*" (deposition by Perrenet at the trial of the *coquillards*).

By simply putting the sources related to these two events side by side, Alice Becker-Ho has been able to realize the Benjaminian project of writing an original work composed mostly of quotations.[2] The book's thesis is apparently anodyne: as the subtitle indicates — *A neglected factor at the origins of the argot of the dangerous classes* — the question consists in demonstrating the derivation of part of the *argot* lexicon from *Rom,* the language of Gypsies. A brief but essential glossary at the end of the volume lists those argotic terms that have "an evident echo, not to say a sure origin, in the Gypsy dialects of Europe."[3]

Although this thesis does not exceed the boundaries of sociolinguistics, it implies nonetheless another and more significant argument: as much as *argot* is not properly a language but a jargon, so the Gypsies are not a people but the last descendants of a class of outlaws dating from another era:

> Gypsies are our Middle Ages preserved; dangerous classes of an earlier epoch. The Gypsy terms that made it into the different *argots* are much like the Gypsies themselves: since their first apparence, in fact, Gypsies adopted the patronymics of the countries through which they traveled—*gadjesko nav*—thereby losing somehow their identity on paper in the eyes of all those who believe they can read.[4]

This explains why scholars were never successful in interpreting the Gypsies' origins and in getting to know well their language and customs: the ethnographic investigation, in this case, becomes impossible because the informers are systematically lying.

Why is this most original hypothesis—which refers, after all, to marginal linguistic realities and to marginal populations—so important? Benjamin once wrote that, at crucial moments of history, the final blow must be struck with the left hand, intervening on the hidden nuts and bolts of the machine of social knowledge. Although Alice Becker-Ho maintains herself within the limits of her thesis, it is probable that she is perfectly aware of having laid a mine—which is ready to explode at any given time—at the very focal point of our political theory. We do not have, in fact, the slighest idea of what either a people or a language is. (It is well known that linguists can construct a grammar—that is, a unitary system with describable characteristics that could be called language—only by taking the *factum loquendi* for granted, that is, only by taking for granted the simple fact that human beings speak and understand each other, a fact that is still inaccessible to science.) Nevertheless, all of our political culture is based on the relation between these two notions. Romantic ideology—which consciously created this connection, thereby influencing extensively modern linguistic theory as well as the political theory that is still dominant nowadays—tried to clarify something that was already obscure (the concept of people) with the help of something even more obscure (the concept of language). Thanks to the symbiotic correspondence thus instituted, two contingent and indefinite cultural entities transform themselves into almost natural organisms endowed with their own necessary laws and characteristics. Political theory, in fact, must presuppose, without the ability to explain it, the *factum pluralitatis*—a term etymologically related to *populus*, with which I would like to indicate the simple fact that human beings form a community—whereas linguistics must presuppose, without questioning it, the *factum loquendi*. The simple correspondence between these two facts defines modern political discourse.

The relation between Gypsies and *argot* puts this correspondence radically into question in the very instant in which it parodically reenacts it. Gypsies are to a people what *argot* is to language. And although this analogy can last but for a brief moment, it nonetheless sheds light on that truth which the correspondence between language and people was secretly intended to conceal: all peoples are gangs and *coquilles*, all languages are jargons and *argot*.

What is at stake here is not to evaluate the scientific accuracy of this thesis but rather not to let its liberating power slip out of our hands. Once our gaze is focused on this matter, the perverse and tenacious machines that govern our political imaginary suddenly lose their power. It should be evident to everybody, after all, that we are talking about an imaginary, especially nowadays when the idea of a people has long lost any substantial reality. Even if we admit that this idea never had any real content other than the insipid catalog of characteristics listed by the old philosophical anthropologies, it was already made meaningless, in any case, by the same modern state that presented itself as its keeper and its expression. All well-meaning chatter notwithstanding, the idea of a people today is nothing other than the empty support of state identity and is recognized only as such. For those who might still nurture some doubt on the matter, it would be instructive to take a look at what is happening around us from this point of view: on the one hand, the world powers take up arms to defend a *state without a people* (Kuwait) and, on the other hand, the *peoples without a state* (Kurds, Armenians, Palestinians, Basques, Jews of the Diaspora) can be oppressed and exterminated with impunity, so as to make clear that the destiny of a people can only be a state identity and that the concept of *people* makes sense only if recodified within the concept of citizenship. In this regard, it is also important to note the peculiar status of those languages that have no state dignity (Catalan, Basque, Gaelic, etc.), which linguists treat naturally as languages, but which practically operate rather as jargons or dialects and almost always assume an immediately political significance. The vicious entwining of language, people, and the state appears particularly evident in the case of Zionism. A movement that wanted to constitute the people par excellence (Israel) as a state took it upon itself, for this very reason, to reactualize a purely cult language (Hebrew) that had been replaced in daily use by other languages and dialects (Ladino, Yiddish). In the eyes of the keepers of tradition, however, precisely this reactualization of the sacred language appeared to be a grotesque profanity, upon which language would have taken revenge one day. (On December 26, 1926, Gershom Scholem writes to Franz Rosenzweig from Jerusalem: "We live in our language like blind men walking on the edge of an abyss.... This language is laden with future catastrophes.... The day will come when it will turn against those who speak it.")[5]

The thesis according to which all peoples are Gypsies and all languages are jargons untangles this knot and enables us to look in a new way at those linguistic experiences that have periodically emerged within our culture only to be misunderstood and led back to dominant conceptions. What else can Dante mean, in fact, when he says — while narrating the myth of Babel in *De vulgari eloquentia* — that every kind of tower-builder received its own language, which was incomprehensible to the others, and that the languages spoken in his time derived from these Babelic languages? He is presenting all the languages of the Earth as jargons (the language of a trade, in fact, is the figure of jargon par excellence). And against this intimate aptitude for jargon that every language possesses, he does not suggest the remedy of a national language and grammar (as a long-standing falsification of his thought would have it); he suggests, rather, a transformation of the very way of experiencing words, which he called *volgare illustre*. Such a transformation was to be something like a deliverance of the jargons themselves that would direct them toward the *factum loquendi* — and hence not a grammatical deliverance, but a poetical and a political one.

The *trobar clus* of the Provençal troubadours is itself, in a certain way, the transformation of the language *d'oc* into a secret jargon (in a way not so different from that of Villon when he wrote some of his ballads in the *argot* of the *coquillards*). But what this jargon speaks of is nothing more than another figure of language, marked as the place and the object of a love experience. From this point of view, it is not surprising that, in more recent debates, the experience of the pure existence of language (that is, the experience of the *factum loquendi*) could coincide, according to Wittgenstein, with ethics;

nor is it surprising that Benjamin could entrust the figure of redeemed humanity to a "pure language" that was irreducible to a grammar or to a particular language.

Languages are the jargons that hide the pure experience of language just as peoples are the more or less successful masks of the *factum pluralitatis*. This is why our task cannot possibly be either the construction of these jargons into grammars or the recodification of peoples into state identities. On the contrary, it is only by breaking at any point the nexus between the existence of language, grammar, people, and state that thought and praxis will be equal to the tasks at hand. The forms of this interruption—during which the *factum* of language and the *factum* of community come to light for an instant—are manifold and change according to times and circumstances: reactivation of a jargon, *trobar clus*, pure language, minoritarian practice of a grammatical language, and so on. In any case, it is clear that what is at stake here is not something simply linguistic or literary but, above all, political and philosophical.

(1995)

Marginal Notes on Commentaries on the Society of the Spectacle

Strategist

GUY DEBORD's books constitute the clearest and most severe analysis of the miseries and slavery of a society that by now has extended its dominion over the whole planet—that is to say, the society of the spectacle in which we live. As such, these books do not need clarifications, praises, or, least of all, prefaces. At most it might be possible to suggest here a few glosses in the margins, much like those signs that the medieval copyists traced alongside of the most noteworthy passages. Following a rigorous anchoritic intention, they are in fact *separated* from the text and they find their own place not in an improbable elsewhere, but solely in the precise cartographic delimitation of what they describe.

It would be of no use to praise these books' independence of judgment and prophetic clairvoyance, or the classic perspicuity of their style. There are no authors today who could console themselves by thinking that their work will be read in a century (by *what kind* of human beings?), and there are no readers who could flatter themselves (with respect to what?) with the knowledge of belonging to that small number of people who understood that work before others did. They should be used rather as manuals, as instruments of resistance or exodus—much like those improper weapons that the fugitive picks up and inserts hastily under the belt (according to a beautiful image of Deleuze). Or, rather, they should be used as the work of a peculiar strategist (the title *Commentaries*, in fact, harks back to a tradition of this kind)— a strategist whose field of action is not so much a battle in which to marshal troops but the pure power of the intellect. A sentence by Karl von Clausewitz, cited in the fourth Italian edition of *The Society of the Spectacle*, expresses perfectly this character:

> In strategic critiques, the essential fact is to position yourself exactly in the actors' point of view. It is true that this is often very difficult. Most strategic critiques would disappear completely or would be reduced to minor differences of understanding if the writers would or could position themselves in all the circumstances in which the actors had found themselves.[1]

In this sense, not only Machiavelli's *The Prince* but also Spinoza's *Ethics* are treatises on strategy: operations *de potentia intellectus, sive de libertate*.

Phantasmagoria

Marx was in London when the first Universal Exposition was inaugurated with enormous clamor in Hyde Park in 1851. Among the various projects submitted, the organizers had chosen the one by Paxton, which called for an immense building made entirely of crystal. In the Exposition's catalog, Merrifield wrote that the Crystal Palace "is perhaps the only building in the world in which the atmosphere is perceivable ... by a spectator situated either at the west or east extremity of the gallery ... where the most distant parts of the building appear wrapped in a light blue halo."[2] The first great triumph of the commodity thus takes place under the sign of both transparency and phantasmagoria. Furthermore, the guide to the Paris Universal Exposition of 1867 reinstates this contradictory spectacular character: "Il faut au [public] une conception grandiose qui frappe son imagination ... il veut contempler un coup d'œil féerique et non pas des produits similaires et uniformement groupés" [The public needs a grandiose conception that strikes its imagination ... it wants to behold a wondrous prospect rather than similar and uniformly arranged products].

It is probable that Marx had in mind the impression felt in the Crystal Palace when he wrote the chapter of *Capital* on commodity fetishism. It is certainly not a coincidence that this chapter occupies a liminal position. The disclosure of the commodity's "secret" was the key that revealed capital's enchanted realm to our thought—a secret that capital always tried to hide by exposing it in full view.

Without the identification of this immaterial center—in which "the products of labor" split themselves into a use value and an exchange value and "become commodities, sensuous things which are at the same

time suprasensible or social"[3] — all the following criti-
cal investigations undertaken in *Capital* probably would
not have been possible.

In the 1960s, however, the Marxian analysis of
the fetish character of the commodity was, in the Marx-
ist milieu, foolishly abandoned. In 1969, in the preface
to a popular reprint of *Capital*, Louis Althusser could still
invite readers to skip the first section, with the reason
that the theory of fetishism was a "flagrant" and "ex-
tremely harmful" trace of Hegelian philosophy.[4]

It is for this reason that Debord's gesture appears all the more remarkable, as he bases his analysis
of the society of the spectacle — that is, of a capitalism
that has reached its extreme figure — precisely on that
"flagrant trace." The "becoming-image" of capital is
nothing more than the commodity's last metamorphosis, in which exchange value has completely eclipsed use
value and can now achieve the status of absolute and ir-
responsible sovereignty over life in its entirety, after having falsified the entire social production. In this sense,
the Crystal Palace in Hyde Park, where the commodity
unveiled and exhibited its mystery for the first time, is a
prophecy of the spectacle, or, rather, the nightmare, in
which the nineteenth century dreamed the twentieth.
The first duty the Situationists assigned themselves was
to wake up from this nightmare.

Walpurgis Night

If there is in our century a writer with whom Debord
might agree to be compared, this writer would be Karl

Kraus. Nobody has been able to bring to light the hidden laws of the spectacle as Kraus did in his obstinate struggle against journalists — "in these loud times which boom with the horrible symphony of actions which produce reports and of reports which cause actions."[5] And if someone were to imagine something analogous to the voice-over that in Debord's films runs alongside the exposure of that desert of rubble which is the spectacle, nothing would be more appropriate than Kraus's voice. A voice that — in those public lectures whose charm Elias Canetti has described — finds and lays bare the intimate and ferocious anarchy of triumphant capitalism in Offenbach's operetta.

The punch line with which Kraus, in the posthumous *Third Walpurgis Night*, justified his silence in the face of the rise of Nazism is well known: "On Hitler, nothing comes to my mind." This ferocious *Witz*, where Kraus confesses without indulgence his own limitation, marks also the impotence of satire when faced by the becoming-reality of the indescribable. As a satirical poet, he is truly "only one of the last epigones inhabiting the ancient home of language." Certainly also in Debord, as much as in Kraus, language presents itself as the image and the place of justice. Nevertheless, the analogy stops there. Debord's discourse begins precisely where satire becomes speechless. The ancient home of language (as well as the literary tradition on which satire is based) has been, by now, falsified and manipulated from top to bottom. Kraus reacts to this situation by turning language into the place of Universal Judgment. Debord begins to speak instead when the Universal Judgment has already taken place and after the true has been recognized in it only as a moment of the false. The Universal Judgment in language and the Walpurgis Night in the spectacle coincide perfectly. This paradoxical coincidence is the place from which perennially resounds his voice-over.

Situation

What is a constructed situation? A definition contained in the first issue of the *Internationale Situationniste* states that this is a moment in life, concretely and deliberately constructed through the collective organization of a unified milieu and through a play of events. Nothing would be more misleading, however, than to think the situation as a privileged or exceptional moment in the sense of aestheticism. The situation is neither the becoming-art of life nor the becoming-life of art. We can comprehend its true nature only if we locate it historically in its proper place: that is, *after* the end and self-destruction of art, and *after* the passage of life through the trial of nihilism. The "Northwest passage of the geography of the true life" is a point of indifference between life and art, where *both* undergo a decisive metamorphosis *simultaneously*. This point of indifference constitutes a politics that is finally adequate to its tasks. The Situationists counteract capitalism—which "concretely and deliberately" organizes environments and events in order to depotentiate life—with a concrete, although opposite, project. Their utopia is, once again, perfectly topical because it locates itself in the taking-place of what it wants to overthrow. Nothing could give a better idea of a constructed situation, perhaps, than the bare scenography in which Nietzsche, in *The Gay Science*, develops his thought's *experimentum crucis*. A constructed situation is the room with the spider and the moonlight between the branches exactly in the moment when—in answer to the demon's question: "Do you desire this once more and innumerable times more?"—it is said: "Yes, I do."[6] What is decisive here is the messianic shift that *integrally* changes the world, leaving it, at the same time, *almost* intact: everything here, in fact, stayed the same, but lost its identity.

In the commedia dell'arte there were cadres— instructions meant for the actors, so that they would bring into being situations in which a human gesture, subtracted from the powers of myth and destiny, could finally take place. It is impossible to understand the comic mask if we simply interpret it as an undetermined or depotentiated character. Harlequin and the Doctor are not characters in the same way in which Hamlet and Oedipus are: the masks are not *characters*, but rather *gestures* figured as a type, constellations of gestures. In this situation, the destruction of the role's identity goes hand in hand with the destruction of the actor's identity. It is precisely this relationship between text and execution, between power and act, that is put into question once again here. This happens because the mask insinuates itself between the text and the execution, creating an indistinguishable mixture of power and act. And what takes place here — both onstage and within the constructed situation — is not the actuation of a power but the liberation of an ulterior power. *Gesture* is the name of this intersection between life and art, act and power, general and particular, text and execution. It is a moment of life subtracted from the context of individual biography as well as a moment of art subtracted from the neutrality of aesthetics: it is pure praxis. The gesture is neither use value nor exchange value, neither biographic experience nor impersonal event: it is the other side of the commodity that lets the "crystals of this common social substance" sink into the situation.

Auschwitz/Timisoara

Probably the most disquieting aspect of Debord's books is the fact that history seems to have committed itself to relentlessly confirm their analyses. Twenty years after *The Society of the Spectacle*, the *Commentaries* (1988) registered the precision of the diagnosis and expectations of that previous book in every aspect. Meanwhile, the course of history has accelerated uniformly in the same direction: only two years after this book's publication, in fact, we could say that world politics is nothing more than a hasty and parodic mise-en-scène of the script contained in that book. The substantial unification of the concentrated spectacle (the Eastern people's democracies) and of the diffused spectacle (the Western democracies) into an integrated spectacle is, by now, trivial evidence. This unification, which constituted one of the central theses of the *Commentaries*, appeared paradoxical to many people at the time. The immovable walls and the iron curtains that divided the two worlds were wiped out in a few days. The Eastern governments allowed the Leninist party to fall so that the integrated spectacle could be completely realized in their countries. In the same way, the West had already renounced a while ago the balance of powers as well as real freedom of thought and communication in the name of the electoral machine of majority vote and of media control over public opinion—both of which had developed within the totalitarian modern states.

Timisoara, Romania, represents the extreme point of this process, and deserves to give its name to the new turn in world politics. Because there the secret police had conspired against itself in order to overthrow the old spectacle-concentrated regime while television showed, nakedly and without false modesty, the real political function of the media. Both television and secret police, therefore, succeeded in doing something that Nazism had not even dared to imagine: to bring Auschwitz and the Reichstag fire together in one monstrous event. For the first time in the history of humankind, corpses that had just been buried or lined up on the morgue's tables were hastily exhumed and tortured in order to simulate, in front of the video cameras, the genocide that legitimized the new regime. What the entire world was watching live on television, thinking it was the real truth, was in reality the absolute nontruth; and, although the falsification appeared to be sometimes quite obvious, it was nevertheless legitimized as true by the media's world system, so that it would be clear that the true was, by now, nothing more than a moment within the necessary movement of the false. In this way, truth and falsity became indistinguishable from each other and the spectacle legitimized itself solely through the spectacle.

Timisoara is, in this sense, the Auschwitz of the age of the spectacle: and in the same way in which it has been said that after Auschwitz it is impossible to write and think as before, after Timisoara it will be no longer possible to watch television in the same way.

Shekinah

How can thought collect Debord's inheritance today, in the age of the complete triumph of the spectacle? It is evident, after all, that the spectacle is language, the very communicativity and linguistic being of humans. This means that an integrated Marxian analysis should take into consideration the fact that capitalism (or whatever other name we might want to give to the process dominating world history today) not only aimed at the expropriation of productive activity, but also, and above all, at the alienation of language itself, of the linguistic and communicative nature of human beings, of that *logos* in which Heraclitus identifies the Common. The extreme form of the expropriation of the Common is the spectacle, in other words, the politics in which we live. But this also means that what we encounter in the spectacle is our very linguistic nature inverted. For this reason (precisely because what is being expropriated is the possibility itself of a common good), the spectacle's violence is so destructive; but, for the same reason, the spectacle still contains something like a positive possibility — and it is our task to use this possibility against it.

Nothing resembles this condition more than the sin that cabalists call "isolation of the Shekinah" and that they attribute to Aher — one of the four rabbis who, according to a famous Haggadah of the Talmud, entered the Pardes (that is, supreme knowledge). "Four rabbis," the story goes, "entered Heaven: Ben Azzai, Ben Zoma, Aher and Rabbi Akiba.... Ben Azzai cast a glance and died.... Ben Zoma looked and went crazy.... Aher cut the branches. Rabbi Akiba came out uninjured."

The Shekinah is the last of the ten Sefirot or attributes of the divinity, the one that expresses divine presence itself, its manifestation or habitation on Earth: its "word." Aher's "cutting of the branches" is identified by cabalists with the sin of Adam, who, instead of contemplating the Sefirot in their totality, preferred to contemplate only the last one, isolating it from the others — thereby separating the tree of science from the tree of life. Like Adam, Aher represents humanity insofar as, making knowledge his own destiny and his own specific power, he isolates knowledge and the word, which are nothing other than the most complete form of the manifestation of God (the Shekinah), from the other Sefirot in which he reveals himself. *The risk here is that the word — that is, the nonlatency and the revelation of something — might become separate from what it reveals and might end up acquiring an autonomous consistency.* The revealed and manifested—and hence, common and share-able—being becomes separate from the thing revealed and comes in between the latter and human beings. In this condition of exile, the Shekinah loses its positive power and becomes harmful (the cabalists say that it "sucks the milk of evil").

The isolation of the Shekinah thus expresses our epochal condition. Whereas under the old regime the estrangement of the communicative essence of human beings substantiated itself as a presupposition that served as the common foundation, in the society of the specta-cle it is this very communicativity, this generic essence itself (that is, language as *Gattungswesen*), that is being separated in an autonomous sphere. What prevents com-munication is communicability itself; human beings are kept separate by what unites them. Journalists and the media establishment (as well as psychoanalysts in the pri-vate sphere) constitute the new clergy of such an alien-ation of the linguistic nature of human beings.

In the society of the spectacle, in fact, the iso-lation of the Shekinah reaches its final phase, in which language not only constitutes itself as an autonomous sphere, but also no longer reveals anything at all—or, better yet, it reveals the nothingness of all things. In lan-guage there is nothing of God, of the world, of the re-vealed: but, in this extreme nullifying unveiling, language (the linguistic nature of human beings) remains once again hidden and separated. Language thus acquires, for the last time, the unspoken power to claim a historical age and a state for itself: the age of the spectacle, or the state of fully realized nihilism. This is why today power founded on a presupposed foundation is vacillating all around the planet: the kingdoms of the Earth are setting out, one after the other, for the spectacular-democratic regime that constitutes the completion of the state-form. Even more than economic necessities and technological development, what drives the nations of the Earth toward a single common destiny is the alienation of linguistic being, the uprooting of all peoples from their vital dwelling in language. But exactly for this reason, the age in which we live is also that in which for the first time it becomes possible for human beings to experience their own linguistic essence — to experience, that is, not some language content or some true proposition, but language *itself*, as well as the very fact of speaking. Contemporary politics is precisely this devastating *experimentum linguae* that disarticulates and empties, all over the planet, traditions and beliefs, ideologies and religions, identities and communities.

Only those who will be able to carry it to completion — without allowing that which reveals to be veiled in the nothingness it reveals, but bringing language itself to language — will become the first citizens of a community with neither presuppositions nor a state. In this community, the nullifying and determining power of what is common will be pacified and the Shekinah will no longer suck the evil milk of its own separateness. Like Rabbi Akiba in the Haggadah of the Talmud, the citizens of this community will enter the paradise of language and will come out of it uninjured.

Tiananmen

What does the scenario that world politics is setting up before us look like under the twilight of the *Commentaries*? The state of the integrated spectacle (or, spectacular-democratic state) is the final stage in the evolution of the state-form — the ruinous stage toward which monarchies and republics, tyrannies and democracies, racist regimes and progressive regimes are all rushing. Although it seems to bring national identities back to life, this global movement actually embodies a tendency toward the constitution of a kind of supranational police state, in which the norms of international law are tacitly abrogated one after the other. Not only has no war officially been declared in many years (confirming Carl Schmitt's prophecy, according to which every war in our time has become a civil war), but even the outright invasion of a sovereign state can now be presented as an act of internal jurisdiction. Under these circumstances, the secret services — which had always been used to act ignoring the boundaries of national sovereignties — become the model itself of real political organization and of real political action. For the first time in the history of our century, the two most important world powers are headed by two direct emanations of the secret services: Bush (former CIA head) and Gorbachev (Andropov's man); and the more they concentrate all the power in their own hands, the more all of this is hailed, in the new course of the spectacle, as a triumph of democracy. All appearances notwithstanding, the spectacular-democratic world organization that is thus emerging actually runs the risk of being the worst tyranny that ever materialized in the history of humanity, against which resistance and dissent will be practically more and more difficult—and all the more so in that it is increasingly clear that such an organization will have the task of managing *the survival of humanity in an uninhabitable world.* One cannot be sure, however, that the spectacle's attempt to maintain control over the process it contributed to putting in motion in the first place will actually succeed. The state of the spectacle, after all, is still a state that bases itself (as Badiou has shown every state to base itself) not on social bonds, of which it purportedly is the expression, but rather on their dissolution, which it forbids. In the final analysis, the state can recognize any claim for identity—even that of a state identity within itself (and in our time, the history of the relations between the state and terrorism is an eloquent confirmation of this fact). But what the state cannot tolerate in any way is that singularities form a community without claiming an identity, that human beings co-belong without a representable condition of belonging (being Italian, working-class, Catholic, terrorist, etc.). And yet, the state of the spectacle—inasmuch as it empties and nullifies every real identity, and substitutes the *public* and *public opinion* for the *people* and the *general will*—is precisely what produces massively from within itself singularities that are no longer characterized either by any social identity or by any real condition of belonging: singularities that are truly *whatever* singularities. It is clear that the society of the spectacle is also one in which all social identities have dissolved and in which everything that for centuries represented the splendor and misery of the generations succeeding themselves on Earth has by now lost all its significance. The different identities that have marked the tragicomedy of universal history are exposed and gathered with a phantasmagorical vacuity in the global petite bourgeoisie — a petite bourgeoisie that constitutes the form in which the spectacle has realized parodistically the Marxian project of a classless society.

For this reason — to risk advancing a prophecy here — the coming politics will no longer be a struggle to conquer or to control the state on the part of either new or old social subjects, but rather a struggle between the state and the nonstate (humanity), that is, an irresolvable disjunction between whatever singularities and the state organization.

This has nothing to do with the mere demands of society against the state, which was for a long time the shared concern of the protest movements of our age. Whatever singularities cannot form a *societas* within a society of the spectacle because they do not possess any identity to vindicate or any social bond whereby to seek recognition. The struggle against the state, therefore, is all the more implacable, because this is a state that nullifies all real contents but that — all empty declarations about the sacredness of life and about human rights aside — would also declare any being radically lacking a representable identity to be simply nonexistent.

This is the lesson that could have been learned from Tiananmen, if real attention had been paid to the facts of that event. What was most striking about the demonstrations of the Chinese May, in fact, was the relative absence of specific contents in their demands. (The notions of democracy and freedom are too generic to constitute a real goal of struggle, and the only concrete demand, the rehabilitation of Hu Yaobang, was promptly granted.) It is for this reason that the violence of the state's reaction seems all the more inexplicable. It is likely, however, that this disproportion was only apparent and that the Chinese leaders acted, from their point of view, with perfect lucidity. In Tiananmen the state found itself facing something that could not and did not want to be represented, but that presented itself nonetheless as a community and as a common life (and this regardless of whether those who were in that square were actually aware of it). The threat the state is not willing to come to terms with is precisely the fact that the unrepresentable should exist and form a community without either presuppositions or conditions of belonging (just like Cantor's inconsistent multiplicity). The whatever singularity—this singularity that wants to take possession of belonging itself as well as of its own being-into-language, and that thus declines any identity and any condition of belonging—is the new, nonsubjective, and socially inconsistent protagonist of the coming politics. Wherever these singularities peacefully manifest their being-in-common, there will be another Tiananmen and, sooner or later, the tanks will appear again.

(1990)

The Face

ALL LIVING beings are in the open: they manifest themselves and shine in their appearance. But only human beings want to take possession of this opening, to seize hold of their own appearance and of their own being-manifest. Language is this appropriation, which transforms nature into *face*. This is why appearance becomes a problem for human beings: it becomes the location of a struggle for truth.

The face is at once the irreparable being-exposed of humans and the very opening in which they hide and stay hidden. The face is the only location of community, the only possible city. And that is because that which in single individuals opens up to the political is the tragicomedy of truth, in which they always already fall and out of which they have to find a way.

What the face exposes and reveals is not *something* that could be formulated as a signifying proposition of sorts, nor is it a secret doomed to remain forever incommunicable. The face's revelation is revelation of language itself. Such a revelation, therefore, does not have any real content and does not tell the truth about this or that state of being, about this or that aspect of human beings and of the world: it is *only* opening, *only* communicability. To walk in the light of the face means *to be* this opening — and to suffer it, and to endure it.

Thus, the face is, above all, the *passion* of revelation, the passion of language. Nature acquires a face precisely in the moment it feels that it is being revealed by language. And nature's being exposed and betrayed by the word, its veiling itself behind the impossibility of having a secret, appears on its face as either chastity or perturbation, as either shamelessness or modesty.

The face does not coincide with the visage. There is a face wherever something reaches the level of exposition and tries to grasp its own being exposed, wherever a being that appears sinks in that appearance and has to find a way out of it. (Thus, art can give a face even to an inanimate object, to a still nature; and that is why the witches, when accused by the inquisitors of kissing Satan's anus during the Sabbath, argued that even there there was a face. And it may be that nowadays the entire Earth, which has been transformed into a desert by humankind's blind will, might become one single face.)

I look someone in the eyes: either these eyes are cast down — and this is modesty, that is, modesty for the emptiness lurking behind the gaze — or they look back at me. And they can look at me shamelessly, thereby exhibiting their own emptiness as if there was another abyssal eye behind it that knows this emptiness and uses it as an impenetrable hiding place. Or, they can look at me with a chaste impudence and without reserve, thereby letting love and the word happen in the emptiness of our gazes.

Exposition is the location of politics. If there is no animal politics, that is perhaps because animals are always already in the open and do not try to take possession of their own exposition; they simply live in it without caring about it. That is why they are not interested in mirrors, in the image as image. Human beings, on the other hand, separate images from things and give them a name precisely because they want to recognize themselves, that is, they want to take possession of their own very appearance. Human beings thus transform the open into a world, that is, into the battlefield of a political struggle without quarter. This struggle, whose object is truth, goes by the name of History.

It is happening more and more often that in pornographic photographs the portrayed subjects, by a calculated stratagem, look into the camera, thereby exhibiting the awareness of being exposed to the gaze. This unexpected gesture violently belies the fiction that is implicit in the consumption of such images, according to which the one who looks surprises the actors while remaining unseen by them: the latter, rather, knowingly challenge the voyeur's gaze and force him to look them in the eyes. In that precise moment, the insubstantial nature of the human face suddenly comes to light. The fact that the actors look into the camera means that they *show that they are simulating*; nevertheless, they paradoxically appear more real precisely to the extent to which they exhibit this falsification. The same procedure is used today in advertising: the image appears more convincing if it shows openly its own artifice. In both cases, the one who looks is confronted with something that concerns unequivocally the essence of the face, the very structure of truth.

We may call tragicomedy of appearance the fact that the face uncovers only and precisely inasmuch as it hides, and hides to the extent to which it uncovers. In this way, the appearance that ought to have manifested human beings becomes for them instead a resemblance that betrays them and in which they can no longer recognize themselves. Precisely because the face is solely the location of truth, it is also and immediately the location of simulation and of an irreducible impropriety. This does not mean, however, that appearance dissimulates what it uncovers by making it look like what in reality it is not: rather, what human beings truly are is nothing other than this dissimulation and this disquietude within the appearance. Because human beings neither are nor have to be any essence, any nature, or any specific destiny, their condition is the most empty and the most insubstantial of all: it is the truth. What remains hidden from them is not something behind appearance, but rather appearing itself, that is, their being nothing other than a face. The task of politics is to return appearance itself to appearance, to cause appearance itself to appear.

The face, truth, and exposition are today the objects of a global civil war, whose battlefield is social life in its entirety, whose storm troopers are the media, whose victims are all the peoples of the Earth. Politicians, the media establishment, and the advertising industry have understood the insubstantial character of the face and of the community it opens up, and thus they transform it into a miserable secret that they must make sure to control at all costs. State power today is no longer founded on the monopoly of the legitimate use of violence — a monopoly that states share increasingly willingly with other nonsovereign organizations such as the United Nations and terrorist organizations; rather, it is founded above all on the control of appearance (of *doxa*). The fact that politics constitutes itself as an autonomous sphere goes hand in hand with the separation of the face in the world of spectacle — a world in which human communication is being separated from itself. Exposition thus transforms itself into a value that is accumulated in images and in the media, while a new class of bureaucrats jealously watches over its management.

If what human beings had to communicate to each other were always and only something, there would never be politics properly speaking, but only exchange and conflict, signals and answers. But because what human beings have to communicate to each other is above all a pure communicability (that is, language), politics then arises as the communicative emptiness in which the human face emerges as such. It is precisely this empty space that politicians and the media establishment are trying to be sure to control, by keeping it separate in a sphere that guarantees its unseizability and by preventing communicativity itself from coming to light. This means that an integrated Marxian analysis should take into consideration the fact that capitalism (or whatever other name we might want to give to the process dominating world history today) not only was directed to the expropriation of productive activity, but was also and above all directed to the alienation of language itself, of the communicative nature of human beings.

Inasmuch as it is nothing but pure communicability, every human face, even the most noble and beautiful, is always suspended on the edge of an abyss. This is precisely why the most delicate and graceful faces sometimes look as if they might suddenly decompose, thus letting the shapeless and bottomless background that threatens them emerge. But this amorphous background is nothing else than the opening itself and communicability itself inasmuch as they are constituted as their own presuppositions as if they were a thing. The only face to remain uninjured is the one capable of taking the abyss of its own communicability upon itself and of exposing it without fear or complacency.

This is why the face contracts into an expression, stiffens into a character, and thus sinks further and further into itself. As soon as the face realizes that communicability is all that it is and hence that it has nothing to express — thus withdrawing silently behind itself, inside its own mute identity — it turns into a grimace, which is what one calls character. Character is the constitutive reticence that human beings retain in the word; but what one has to take possession of here is only a nonlatency, a pure visibility: simply a visage. The face is not something that transcends the visage: it is the exposition of the visage in all its nudity, it is a victory over character — it is word.

Everything for human beings is divided between proper and improper, true and false, possible and real: this is because they are or have to be only a face. Every appearance that manifests human beings thus becomes for them improper and factitious, and makes them confront the task of turning truth into their *own proper* truth. But truth itself is not something of which we can take possession, nor does it have any object other than appearance and the improper: it is simply their comprehension, their exposition. The totalitarian politics of the modern, rather, is the will to total self-possession: here either the improper extends its own rule everywhere, thanks to an unrestrainable will to falsification and consumption (as happens in advanced industrialized democracies), or the proper demands the exclusion of any impropriety (as happens in the so-called totalitarian states). In both these grotesque counterfeits of the face, the only truly human

possibility is lost: that is, the possibility of taking possession of impropriety as such, of exposing in the face simply your *own proper* impropriety, of walking in the shadow
of its light.

The human face reproduces the duality that constitutes
it within its own structure, that is, the duality of proper
and improper, of communication and communicability,
of potentiality and act. The face is formed by a passive
background on which the active expressive traits emerge:

> Just as the Star mirrors its elements and the combi-
> nation of the elements into one route in its two su-
> perimposed triangles, so too the organs of the coun-
> tenance divide into two levels. For the life-points of
> the countenance are, after all, those points where the
> countenance comes into contact with the world above,
> be it passive or active contact. The basic level is or-
> dered according to the receptive organs; they are the
> face, the mask, namely forehead and cheeks, to which
> belong respectively nose and ears. Nose and ears are
> the organs of pure receptivity.... This first triangle
> is thus formed by the midpoint of the forehead, as
> the dominant point of the entire face, and the mid-
> point of the cheeks. Over it is now imposed a second
> triangle, composed of the organs whose activity quick-
> ens the rigid mask of the first: eyes and mouth.[1]

In advertising and pornography (consumer
society), the eyes and the mouth come to the foreground;
in totalitarian states (bureaucracy), the passive background is dominant (the inexpressive images of tyrants

in their offices). But only the reciprocal game between these two levels constitutes the life of the face.

There are two words in Latin that derive from the Indo-European root meaning "one": *similis*, which expresses resemblance, and *simul*, which means "at the same time." Thus, next to *similitudo* (resemblance) there is *simultas*, that is, the fact of being together (which implies also rivalry, enmity); and next to *similare* (to be like) there is *simulare* (to copy, to imitate, which implies also to feign, to simulate).

The face is not a *simulacrum*, in the sense that it is something dissimulating or hiding the truth: the face is the *simultas*, the being-together of the manifold visages constituting it, in which none of the visages is truer than any of the others. To grasp the face's truth means to grasp not the *resemblance* but rather the *simultaneity* of the visages, that is, the restless power that keeps them together and constitutes their being-in-common. The face of God, thus, is the *simultas* of human faces: it is "our effigy" that Dante saw in the "living light" of paradise.

My face is my *outside*: a point of indifference with respect to all of my properties, with respect to what is properly one's own and what is common, to what is internal and what is external. In the face, I exist with all of my properties (my being brown, tall, pale, proud, emotional . . .); but this happens without any of these properties essentially identifying me or belonging to me. The face is the threshold of de-propriation and of de-identification of all manners and of all qualities—a threshold in which only the latter become purely communicable. And only where I find a face do I encounter an exteriority and does an *outside* happen to me.

Be only your face. Go to the threshold. Do not remain the subjects of your properties or faculties, do not stay beneath them: rather, go with them, in them, beyond them.

(1995)

PART III

Sovereign Police

ONE OF the least ambiguous lessons learned from the Gulf War is that the concept of sovereignty has been finally introduced into the figure of the police. The nonchalance with which the exercise of a particularly devastating *ius belli* was disguised here as a mere "police operation" cannot be considered to be a cynical mystification (as it was indeed considered by some rightly indignant critics). The most *spectacular* characteristic of this war, perhaps, was that the reasons presented to justify it cannot be put aside as ideological superstructures used to conceal a hidden plan. On the contrary, ideology has in the meantime penetrated so deeply into reality that the declared reasons have to be taken in a rigorously literal sense—particularly those concerning the idea of a new world order. This does not mean, however, that the Gulf War constituted a healthy limitation of state sovereignties because they were forced to serve as policemen for a supranational organism (which is what apologists and extemporaneous jurists tried, in bad faith, to prove).

The point is that the police—contrary to public opinion—are not merely an administrative function of law enforcement; rather, the police are perhaps the place where the proximity and the almost constitutive exchange between violence and right that characterizes the figure of the sovereign is shown more nakedly and clearly than anywhere else. According to the ancient Roman custom, nobody could for any reason come between the consul, who was endowed with imperium, and the lictor closest to him, who carried the sacrificial ax (which was used to perform capital punishment). This contiguity is not coincidental. If the sovereign, in fact, is the one who marks the point of indistinction between violence and right by proclaiming the state of exception and suspending the validity of the law, the police are always operating within a similar state of exception. The rationales of "public order" and "security" on which the police have to decide on a case-by-case basis define an area of indistinction between violence and right that is exactly symmetrical to that of sovereignty. Benjamin rightly noted that:

> The assertion that the ends of police violence are always identical or even connectd to those of general law is entirely untrue. Rather, the "law" of the police really marks the point at which the state, whether from impotence or because of the immanent con-

nections within any legal system, can no longer guarantee through the legal system the empirical ends that it desires at any price to attain.[1]

Hence the display of weapons that characterizes the police in all eras. What is important here is not so much the threat to those who infringe on the right, but rather the display of that sovereign violence to which the bodily proximity between consul and lictor was witness. The display, in fact, happens in the most peaceful of public places and, in particular, during official ceremonies.

This embarrassing contiguity between sovereignty and police function is expressed in the intangible sacredness that, according to the ancient codes, the figure of the sovereign and the figure of the executioner have in common. This contiguity has never been so self-evident as it was on the occasion of a fortuitous encounter that took place on July 14, 1418: as we are told by a chronicler, the Duke of Burgundy had just entered Paris as a conqueror at the head of his troops when, on the street, he came across the executioner Coqueluche, who had been working very hard for him during those days. According to the story, the executioner, who was covered in blood, approached the sovereign and, while reaching for his hand, shouted: "Mon beau frère!"

The entrance of the concept of sovereignty in the figure of the police, therefore, is not at all reassuring. This is proven by a fact that still surprises historians of the Third Reich, namely, that the extermination of the Jews was conceived from the beginning to the end exclusively as a police operation. It is well known that not a single document has ever been found that recognizes the genocide as a decision made by a sovereign organ: the only document we have, in this regard, is the record of a conference that was held on January 20, 1942, at the Grosser Wannsee, and that gathered middle-level and lower-level police officers. Among them, only the name of Adolf Eichmann — head of division B-4 of the Fourth Section of the Gestapo — is noticeable. The extermination of the Jews could be so methodical and deadly only because it was conceived and carried out as a police operation; but, conversely, it is precisely because the genocide was a "police operation" that today it appears, in the eyes of civilized humanity, all the more barbaric and ignominious.

Furthermore, the investiture of the sovereign as policeman has another corollary: it makes it necessary to criminalize the adversary. Schmitt has shown how, according to European public law, the principle *par in parem non habet iurisdictionem* eliminated the possibility that sovereigns of enemy states could be judged as criminals. The declaration of war did not use to imply the suspension of either this principle or the conventions that guaranteed that a war against an enemy who was granted equal dignity would take place according to precise regulations (one of which was the sharp distinction between the army and the civilian population). What we have witnessed with our own eyes from the end of World War I onward is instead a process by which the enemy is first of all excluded from civil humanity and branded as a criminal; only in a second moment does it become possible and licit to eliminate the enemy by a "police operation." Such an operation is not obliged to respect any juridical rule and can thus make no distinctions between the civilian population and soldiers, as well as between the people and their criminal sovereign, thereby returning to the most archaic conditions of belligerence. Sovereignty's gradual slide toward the darkest areas of police law, however, has at least one positive aspect that is worthy of mention here. What the heads of state, who rushed to criminalize the enemy with such zeal, have not yet realized is that this criminalization can at any moment be turned against them. *There is no head of state on Earth today who, in this sense, is not virtually a criminal.* Today, those who should happen to wear the sad redingote of sovereignty know that they may be treated as criminals one day by their colleagues. And certainly we will not be the ones to pity them. The sovereigns who willingly agreed to present themselves as cops or executioners, in fact, now show in the end their original proximity to the criminal.

(1991)

Notes on Politics

THE FALL of the Soviet Communist Party and the unconcealed rule of the capitalist-democratic state on a planetary scale have cleared the field of the two main ideological obstacles hindering the resumption of a political philosophy worthy of our time: Stalinism on one side, and progressivism and the constitutional state on the other. Thought thus finds itself, for the first time, facing its own task without any illusion and without any possible alibi. The "great transformation" constituting the final stage of the state-form is thus taking place before our very eyes: this is a transformation that is driving the kingdoms of the Earth (republics and monarchies, tyrannies and democracies, federations and national states) one after the other toward the state of the integrated spectacle (Guy Debord) and toward "capitalist parliamentarianism" (Alain Badiou). In the same way in which the great transformation of the first industrial revolution destroyed the social and political structures as well as the legal categories of the ancien régime, terms such as *sovereignty, right, nation, people, democracy,* and *general will* by now refer to a reality that no longer has anything to do with what these concepts used to designate — and those who continue to use these concepts uncritically literally do not know what they are talking about. Consensus and public opinion have no more to do with the general will than the "international police" that today fight wars have to do with the sovereignty of the *jus publicum Europaeum.* Contemporary politics is this devastating experiment that disarticulates and empties institutions and beliefs, ideologies and religions, identities and communities all throughout the planet, so as then to rehash and reinstate their definitively nullified form.

The coming thought will have thus to try and take seriously the Hegelo-Kojèvian (and Marxian) theme of the end of history as well as the Heideggerian theme of the entrance into *Ereignis* as the end of the history of being. With respect to this problem, the battlefield is divided today in the following way: on one side, there are those who think the end of history without the end of the state (that is, the post-Kojèvian or postmodern theorists of the fulfillment of the historical process of humanity in a homogeneous universal state); on the other side, there are those who think the end of the state without the end of history (that is, progressivists of all sorts). Neither position is equal to its task because to think the extinction

of the state without the fulfillment of the historical telos is as impossible as to think a fulfillment of history in
which the empty form of state sovereignty would continue to exist. Just as the first thesis proves itself to be
completely impotent against the tenacious survival of the
state-form going through an infinite transition, the second thesis clashes against the increasingly powerful resistance of historical instances (of a national, religious,
or ethnic type). The two positions, after all, can coexist
perfectly well thanks to the proliferation of traditional
instances of the state (that is, instances of a historical
type) under the aegis of a technical-juridical organism
with a posthistorical vocation.

  Only a thought capable of thinking the end
of the state and the end of history *at one and the same
time*, and of mobilizing one against the other, is equal
to this task. This is what the late Heidegger tried to address—albeit in an entirely unsatisfactory way—with
the idea of an *Ereignis*, of an ultimate event in which what
is seized and delivered from historical destiny is the being-hidden itself of the historical principle, that is, historicity itself. Simply because history designates the expropriation itself of human nature through a series of
epochs and historical destinies, it does not follow that the
fulfillment and the appropriation of the historical telos
in question indicate that the historical process of humanity has now cohered in a definitive order (whose management can be handed over to a homogeneous universal
state). It indicates, rather, that the anarchic historicity
itself that—having been posited as a presupposition—

destined living human beings to various epochs and historical cultures must now come to thought *as such*. It indicates, in other words, that now human beings take possession of their own historical being, that is, of their own impropriety. The becoming-proper (nature) of the improper (language) cannot be either formalized or recognized according to the dialectic of *Anerkennung* because it is, at the same time, a becoming-improper (language) of the proper (nature).

The appropriation of historicity, therefore, cannot still take a state-form, given that the state is nothing other than the presupposition and the representation of the being-hidden of the historical *archē*. This appropriation, rather, must open the field to a *nonstatal and nonjuridical* politics and human life—a politics and a life that are yet to be entirely thought.

The concepts of *sovereignty* and of *constituent power*, which are at the core of our political tradition, have to be abandoned or, at least, to be thought all over again. They mark, in fact, the point of indifference between right and violence, nature and *logos*, proper and improper, and as such they do not designate an attribute or an organ of the juridical system or of the state; they designate, rather, their own original structure. Sovereignty is the idea of an undecidable nexus between violence and right, between the living and language—a nexus that necessarily takes the paradoxical form of a decision regarding the state of exception (Schmitt) or *ban* (Nancy) in which the law (language) relates to the living by withdrawing from it, by a-*ban*doning it to its own violence and its own irrelatedness. Sacred life — the life that is presupposed and abandoned by the law in the state of exception — is the mute carrier of sovereignty, the real *sovereign subject*.

Sovereignty, therefore, is the guardian who prevents the undecidable threshold between violence and right, nature and language, from coming to light. We have to fix our gaze, instead, precisely on what the statue of Justice (which, as Montesquieu reminds us, was to be veiled at the very moment of the proclamation of the state of exception) was not supposed to see, namely, what nowadays is apparent to everybody: that *the state of exception is the rule*, that naked life is immediately the carrier of the sovereign nexus, and that, as such, it is today abandoned to a kind of violence that is all the more effective for being anonymous and quotidian.

If there is today a social power [*potenza*], it must see its own impotence [*impotenza*] through to the end, it must decline any will to either posit or preserve right, it must break everywhere the nexus between violence and right, between the living and language that constitutes sovereignty.

While the state in decline lets its empty shell survive everywhere as a pure structure of sovereignty and domination, society as a whole is instead irrevocably delivered to the form of consumer society, that is, a society in which the sole goal of production is comfortable living. The theorists of political sovereignty, such as Schmitt, see in all this the surest sign of the end of politics. And the planetary masses of consumers, in fact, do not seem to foreshadow any new figure of the polis (even when they do not simply relapse into the old ethnic and religious ideals).

However, the problem that the new politics is facing is precisely this: is it possible to have a *political* community that is ordered exclusively for the full enjoyment of wordly life? But, if we look closer, isn't this precisely the goal of philosophy? And when modern political thought was born with Marsilius of Padua, wasn't it defined precisely by the recovery to political ends of the Averroist concepts of "sufficient life" and "well-living"? Once again Walter Benjamin, in the "Theologico-Political Fragment," leaves no doubts regarding the fact that "The order of the profane should be erected on the idea of happiness."[1] The definition of the concept of "happy life" remains one of the essential tasks of the coming thought (and this should be achieved in such a way that this concept is not kept separate from ontology, because: "being: we have no experience of it other than living itself").

The "happy life" on which political philosophy should be founded thus cannot be either the naked life that sovereignty posits as a presupposition so as to turn it into its own subject or the impenetrable extraneity of science and of modern biopolitics that everybody today tries in vain to sacralize. This "happy life" should be, rather, an absolutely profane "sufficient life" that has reached the perfection of its own power and of its own communicability—a life over which sovereignty and right no longer have any hold.

The plane of immanence on which the new political experience is constituted is the terminal expropriation of language carried out by the spectacular state. Whereas in the old regime, in fact, the estrangement of the communicative essence of human beings was substantiated as a presupposition that had the function of common ground (nation, language, religion, etc.), in the contemporary state it is precisely this same communicativity, this same generic essence (language), that is constituted as an autonomous sphere to the extent to which it becomes the essential factor of the production cycle. What hinders communication, therefore, is communicability itself: human beings are being separated by what unites them.

This also means, however, that in this way we encounter our own linguistic nature inverted. For this reason (precisely because what is being expropriated here is the possibility itself of the Common), the spectacle's violence is so destructive; but, for the same reason, the spectacle still contains something like a positive possibility—and it is our task to use this possibility against it. The age in which we are living, in fact, is also the age in which, for the first time, it becomes possible for human beings to experience their own linguistic essence—to experience, that is, not some language content or some true proposition, but the fact itself of speaking.

The experience in question here does not have any objective content and cannot be formulated as a proposition referring to a state of things or to a historical situation. It does not concern a *state* but an *event* of language; it does not pertain to this or that grammar but—so to speak—to the *factum loquendi* as such. Therefore, this experience must be constructed as an experiment concerning the matter itself of thought, that is, the power of thought (in Spinozan terms: an experiment *de potentia intellectus, sive de libertate*).

What is at stake in this experiment is not at all communication intended as destiny and specific goal of human beings or as the logical-transcendental condition of politics (as it is the case in the pseudophilosophies of communication); what is really at stake, rather, is the only possible material experience of being-generic (that is, experience of "compearance"—as Jean-Luc Nancy suggests—or, in Marxian terms, experience of the General Intellect). That is why the first consequence deriving from this experiment is the subverting of the false alternative between ends and means that paralyzes any ethics and any politics. A finality without means (the good and the beautiful as ends unto themselves), in fact, is just as alienating as a mediality that makes sense only with respect to an end. What is in question in political experience is not a higher end but being-into-language itself as pure mediality, being-into-a-mean as an irreducible condition of human beings. *Politics is the exhibition of a mediality: it is the act of making a means visible as such*. Politics is the sphere neither of an end in itself nor of means subordinated to an end; rather, it is the sphere of a pure mediality without end intended as the field of human action and of human thought.

The second consequence of the *experimentum linguae* is that, above and beyond the concepts of appropriation and expropriation, we need to think, rather, the possibility and the modalities of a *free use*. Praxis and political reflection are operating today exclusively within the dialectic of proper and improper—a dialectic in which either the improper extends its own rule everywhere, thanks to an unrestrainable will to falsification and consumption (as it happens in industrialized democracies), or the proper demands the exclusion of any impropriety (as it happens in integralist and totalitarian states). If instead we define the *common* (or, as others suggest, the *same*) as a point of indifference between the proper and the improper—that is, as something that can never be grasped in terms of either expropriation or appropriation but that can be grasped, rather, only as *use*—the essential political problem then becomes: "How does one use a *common*?" (Heidegger probably had something like this in mind when he formulated his supreme concept as neither appropriation nor expropriation, but as appropriation of an expropriation.)

      The new categories of political thought—inoperative community, compearance, equality, loyalty, mass intellectuality, the coming people, whatever singularity, or however else they might be called—will be able to express the political matter that is facing us only if they are able to articulate the location, the manners, and the meaning of this experience of the event of language intended as free use of the common and as sphere of pure means.

(1992)

In This Exile
(Italian Diary, 1992–94)

WE ARE told that the survivors who came back—and who continue to come back—from the camps had no stories to tell, and that, to the extent to which they had been authentic witnesses, they did not try to communicate what they had lived through, as if they themselves were the first to be seized by doubts regarding the reality of what had befallen them, as if they had somehow mistaken a nightmare for a real event. They knew—and still know—that in Auschwitz or in Omarska they had not become "wiser, better, more profound, more human, or more well disposed toward human beings"; rather, they had come out of the camps stripped naked, hollowed out, and disoriented. And they had no wish to talk about it. All due differences notwithstanding, we too are affected by this sense of suspicion regarding our own witnessing. It seems as if nothing of what we have lived through during these years authorizes us to speak.

Suspicion regarding one's own words arises every time that the distinction between public and private loses its meaning. What exactly did the inhabitants of the camps, in fact, live through? Was it a political-historical event (such as, say, in the case of a soldier who participated in the battle of Waterloo), or was it a strictly private experience? Neither one nor the other. If one was a Jew in Auschwitz or a Bosnian woman in Omarska, one entered the camp as a result not of a political choice but rather of what was most private and incommunicable in oneself, that is, one's blood, one's biological body. But precisely the latter functions now as a decisive political criterion. In this sense, the camp truly is the inaugural site of modernity: it is the first space in which public and private events, political life and biological life, become rigorously indistinguishable. Inasmuch as the inhabitant of the camp has been severed from the political community and has been reduced to naked life (and, moreover, to a life "that does not deserve to be lived"), he or she is an absolutely private person. And yet there is not one single instant in which he or she might be able to find shelter in the realm of the private, and it is precisely this indiscernibility that constitutes the specific anguish of the camp.

Kafka was the first to describe with precision this particular type of site, with which since then we have become perfectly familiar. What makes Joseph K.'s vicissitudes at once so disquieting and comic is the fact that a public event par excellence — a trial — is presented instead as an absolutely private occurrence in which the courtroom borders on the bedroom. This is precisely what makes *The Trial* a prophetic book. And not really — or, not only — as far as the camps are concerned. What did we live through in the 1980s? A delirious and solitary private occurrence? Or, rather, a moment bursting with events and a decisive moment in Italian history as well as in the history of the planet? It is as if all that we have experienced during these years has fallen into an opaque zone of indifference, in which everything becomes confused and unintelligible. Are the events of *Tangentopoli* ["Bribeville"], Italy's protracted corruption scandal, for example, public events or private ones? I confess that it is not clear to me. And if terrorism really was an important moment of our recent political history, how is it possible that it rises now to the surface of conscience only thanks to the interior vicissitudes of some individuals and in the form of repentance, guilt, and conversion? To this slippage of the public into the private corresponds also the spectacular publicization of the private: are the diva's breast cancer or Senna's death public vicissitudes or private ones?[1] And how can one touch the porn star's body, since there is not an inch on it that is not public? And yet it is from such a zone of indifference — in which the actions of human experience are being put on sale — that we ought to start today. And if we are calling this opaque zone of indiscernibility "camp," it is, then, still from the camp that we must begin again.

One hears something being continuously repeated in different quarters: that the situation has reached a limit, that things by now have become intolerable, and that change is necessary. Those who repeat this more than anybody else, however, are the politicians and the press that want to guide change in such a way that in the end nothing really changes. As far as the majority of Italians are concerned, they seem to be watching the intolerable in silence, as if they were spying on it while motionless in front of a large television screen. But what exactly is unbearable today in Italy? It is precisely this silence — that is, the fact that a whole people finds itself speechless before its own destiny — that is above all unbearable. Remember that, whenever you try to speak, you will not be able to resort to any tradition and you will not be able to avail yourself of any of the words that sound so good: freedom, progress, democracy, human rights, constitutional state. You will not even be able to show your credentials of representative of Italian culture or of the European spirit and have them count for anything. You will have to try and describe the intolerable without having anything with which to pull yourself out of it. You will have to remain faithful to that inexplicable silence. You will be able to reply to the unbearableness of that silence only by means immanent to it.

Never has an age been so inclined to put up with anything while finding everything intolerable. The very people who gulp down the unswallowable on a daily basis have this word — *intolerable* — ready-made on their lips every time they have to express their own opinion on whatever problem. Only that when someone actually risks giving a definition, one realizes that what is intolerable in the end is only that human bodies be tortured and hacked to pieces, and hence that, apart from that, one can put up with just about anything.

One of the reasons why Italians are silent today is certainly the noise of the media. As soon as the ancien régime began to crumble, the press and television unanimously revolted against it, even though up to that day they had been the main organizers of consent to the regime. Thus, they literally silenced people, thereby impeding that facts would follow the words that had been recovered slowly and with much effort.

      One of the not-so-secret laws of the spectacular-democratic society in which we live wills it that, whenever power is seriously in crisis, the media establishment apparently dissociates itself from the regime of which it is an integral part so as to govern and direct the general discontent lest it turn itself into revolution. It is not always necessary to simulate an event, as happened in Timisoara; it suffices to anticipate not only facts (by declaring, for example, as many newspapers have been doing for months, that the revolution has already happened), but also citizens' sentiments by giving them expression on the front page of newspapers before they turn into gesture and discourse, and hence circulate and grow through daily conversations and exchanges of opinion. I still remember the paralyzing impression that the word

SHAME as a banner headline on the front page of one of the regime's major dailies made on me the day after the authorization to proceed legally against Bettino Craxi was not granted.[2] To find in the morning the right word to say ready-made on the front page of a newspaper produces a singular effect, a feeling at once of reassurance and of frustration. And a reassuring frustration, that is, the feeling of those who have been dispossessed of their own expressive faculties, is today the dominant affect in Italy.

We Italians live today in a state of absolute absence of legitimacy. The legitimation of nation-states, of course, had been in crisis everywhere for some time, and the most evident symptom of such a crisis was precisely the obsessive attempt to make up in terms of legality, through an unprecedented proliferation of norms and regulations, for what was being lost in terms of legitimacy. But nowhere has decline reached the extreme limit at which we are getting used to living. There is no power or public authority right now that does not nakedly show its own emptiness and its own abjection. The judicial powers have been spared such ruination only because, much like the Erinyes of Greek tragedy that have ended up in a comedy by mistake, they act solely as an instance of punishment and revenge.

This means, however, that Italy is becoming once again the privileged political laboratory that it had been during the 1970s. Just as the governments and services of the entire world had observed then with attentive participation (and that is the least one can say, for they actively collaborated in the experiment) the way that a well-aimed politics of terrorism could possibly function as the mechanism of relegitimation of a discredited system, now the very same eyes watch with curiosity how a constituted power might govern the passage to a new constitution without passing through a constitutive power. Naturally, one is dealing here with a delicate experiment during which it is possible that the patient may not survive (and that would not necessarily be the worst outcome).

In the 1980s, those who spoke of conspiracies were accused of Oldthink. Nowadays, it is the president of the republic himself who publicly denounces the state secret services before the whole country as having conspired, and as continuing to conspire, against the constitution and public order. This accusation is imprecise only with regard to one detail: as someone already has punctually pointed out, all conspiracies in our time are actually *in favor* of the constituted order. And the enormity of such a denunciation is matched only by the brazenness with which the supreme organ of the state admits that its own secret services have made attempts on the life of the citizens, while forgetting to add that this was done for the good of the country and for the security of its public institutions.

The statement released by the head of a large democratic party, according to whom the judges who were indicting him were actually conspiring against themselves, is more impenetrable and yet unwittingly prophetic. During the terminal phase of the evolution of the state-form, each state organ and service is engaged in a ruthless as well as uncontrollable conspiracy against itself and against every other organ and service.

Nowadays one often hears journalists and politicians (and in particular the president of the republic) warning citizens regarding a presumed crisis of the "sense of the state." One used to speak rather of "reason of state" — which Botero had defined without hypocrisy: "State is a stable rule over a people and Reason of State is the knowledge of the means by which such a dominion may be founded, preserved and extended."[3] What is hidden behind this slippage from *reason* to *sense*, from the rational to the irrational? Because it would be simply indecent to speak of "reason of state" today, power looks for one last possibility of well-being in a "sense" that nobody quite understands where it resides and that reminds one of the sense of honor in the ancien régime. But a state that has lost its reason and become insane has also lost its senses and become unconscious. It is now blind and deaf, and it gropes its way toward its own end, heedless of the ruination into which it drags its subjects along.

Of what are Italians repenting?[4] The first to repent were mafiosi and members of the Red Brigades, and since then we have been witnessing an interminable procession of faces that have been grim in their resolve and determined in their very wavering. In the case of the mafiosi, the face would appear in shadow so as to make sure that it would not be recognized, and — as if from the burning bush — we would hear "only a voice." This is the dire voice with which the conscience calls from the shadows nowadays, as if our time did not know any other ethical experience outside of repentance. But this is precisely the point at which our time betrays its inconsistency. Repentance, in fact, is the most treacherous of moral categories — and it is not even clear that it can be counted at all among genuine ethical concepts. It is well known how peremptorily Spinoza bars repentance from any right of citizenship in his *Ethics*. The one who repents — he writes — is twice disgraceful: the first time because he committed an act of which he has had to repent, and the second time because he has repented of it. But repentance presented itself right away as a problem already when it began powerfully to permeate Catholic doctrine and morality in the twelfth century. How does one, in fact, prove the authenticity of repentance? Camps were soon formed with Peter Abelard on one side, whose only requirement was the contrition of the heart, and the "penitentials" on the other side, for whom the unfathomable interior disposition of the one who repents was not important when compared instead to the unequivocal accomplishment of external acts. The whole question thus turned upon itself right away like a vicious circle, in which external acts had to attest to the authenticity of repentance and internal contrition had to guarantee the sincerity of the works. Today's trials function according to the same logic, which decrees that to accuse one's own conceited victories on the misfortunes of the former, for these, no, there truly is no hope.

The icons of the souls of purgatory in the streets of Naples. The large one I saw yesterday near the courthouse had almost all the statuettes of the purgatorial souls with their arms broken off. They were lying on the ground; they were no longer raised high in gestures of invocation — useless emblems of a torture more terrible than fire.

Of what are Italians ashamed? It is striking how frequently in public debates, as well as in the streets or in cafés, as soon as the discussion gets heated up, the expression "Shame on you!" readily comes in handy, almost as if it held the decisive argument every time. Shame, of course, is the prelude to repentance, and repentance in Italy today is the winning card. But none of those who throw shame in other people's faces truly expect them suddenly to blush and declare that they have repented. On the contrary, it is taken for granted that they will not do that. It seems, however, that, in this strange game that everybody here is busy playing, the first ones who succeed in using that formula will have truth on their side. If repentance informs the relationship that Italians have with the good, shame dominates their relation to truth. And if repentance is their only ethical experience, they likewise have no other relation to the true outside of shame. But one is dealing here with a shame that survived those who should have felt it and that has become as objective and impersonal as a juridical truth. In a trial in which repentance has been given the decisive role, shame is the only truth on which judgment might be passed.

Marx still used to put some trust in shame. When Arnold Ruge would object that no revolution has ever come out of shame, Marx would reply that shame already is a revolution, and he defined it as "a sort of anger that turns on itself."[5] But what he was referring to was the "national shame" that concerns specific peoples each with respect to other peoples, the Germans with respect to the French. Primo Levi has shown, however, that there is today a "shame of being human," a shame that in some way or other has tainted every human being. This was — and still is — the shame of the camps, the shame of the fact that what should not have happened did happen. And it is a shame of this type, as it has been rightly pointed out, that we feel today when faced by too great a vulgarity of thought, when watching certain TV shows, when confronted with the faces of their hosts and with the self-assured smiles of those "experts" who jovially lend their qualifications to the political game of the media. Those who have felt this silent shame of being human have also severed within themselves any link with the political power in which they live. Such a shame feeds their thoughts and constitutes the beginning of a revolution and of an exodus of which it is barely able to discern the end.

(At the moment when the executioners' knives are about to penetrate his flesh, Joseph K. with one last leap succeeds in getting hold of the shame that will survive him.)

Nothing is more nauseating than the impudence with which those who have turned money into their only raison d'être periodically wave around the scarecrow of economic crisis: the rich nowadays wear plain rags so as to warn the poor that sacrifices will be necessary *for everybody*. And the docility is just as astonishing; those who have made themselves stolidly complicitous with the imbalance of the public debt, by handing all their savings over to the state in exchange for bonds, now receive the warning blow without batting an eyelash and ready themselves to tighten their belts. And yet those who have any lucidity left in them know that the crisis is always in process and that it constitutes the internal motor of capitalism in its present phase, much as the state of exception is today the normal structure of political power. And just as the state of exception requires that there be increasingly numerous sections of residents deprived of political rights and that in fact at the outer limit all citizens be reduced to naked life, in such a way crisis, having now become permanent, demands not only that the people of the Third World become increasingly poor, but also that a growing percentage of the citizens of the industrialized societies be marginalized and without a job. And there is no so-called democratic state today that is not compromised and up to its neck in such a massive production of human misery.

The punishment for those who go away from love is to be handed over to the power of judgment: they will have to judge one another.

Such is the sense of the rule of the law over human life in our time: all other religious and ethical powers have lost their strength and survive only as indult or suspension of *punishment* and under no circumstances as interruption or refusal of *judgment*. Nothing is more dismal, therefore, than this unconditional being-in-force of juridical categories in a world in which they no longer mirror any comprehensible ethical content: their being-in-force is truly meaningless, much as the countenance of the guardian of the law in Kafka's parable is inscrutable. This loss of sense, which transforms the clearest of sentences into a *non liquet*, explodes and comes into full view with Craxi's confessions and with the confessions of all those who were in power and governed us up until yesterday, precisely when they have to abdicate to others who are probably no better than they were. That is because here to plead guilty is immediately a universal call upon everyone as an accomplice of everybody else, and where everybody is guilty judgment is technically impossible. (Even the Lord on the Last Day would refrain from pronouncing his sentence if everybody had to be damned.) The law here retreats back to its original injunction that — according to the intention of the Apostle Paul — expresses its inner contradiction: *be guilty.*

Nothing manifests the definitive end of the Christian ethics of love intended as a power that unites human beings better than this supremacy of the law. But what betrays itself here is also the church of Christ's unconditional renunciation of any messianic intention. That is because the Messiah is the figure in which religion confronts the problem of the law, in which religion and the law come to the decisive day of reckoning. In the Jewish as much as in the Christian and Shiite contexts, in fact, the messianic event marks first of all a crisis and a radical transformation of the properly legal order of religious tradition. The old law (the Torah of creation) that had been valid up to that moment now ceases to be valid; but obviously, it is not simply a question of substituting for it a new law that would include commandments and prohibitions that would be different from and yet structurally homogeneous with the previous ones. Hence the paradoxes of messianism, which Sabbatai Zevi expressed by saying: "The fulfillment of the Torah is its transgression" and which Christ expressed (more soberly than Paul) in the formula: "I did not come to destroy the law, but to fulfill it."

Having struck with the law a lasting compromise, the church has frozen the messianic event, thereby handing the world over to the power of judgment—a power, however, that the church cunningly manages in the form of the indult and of the penitential remission of sins. (The Messiah has no need for such a remission: the "forgive us our trespasses as we forgive those who trespass against us" is nothing other than the anticipation of the messianic fulfillment of the law.) The task that messianism had assigned to modern politics—to think a human community that would not have (only) the figure of the law — still awaits the minds that might undertake it.

Today, the political parties that define themselves as "progressive" and the so-called leftist coalitions have won in the large cities where there have been elections. One is struck by the victors' excessive preoccupation with presenting themselves as the establishment and with reassuring at all costs the old economic, political, and religious powers. When Napoleon defeated the Mamluks in Egypt, the first thing he did was to summon the notables who constituted the old regime's backbone and to inform them that under the new sovereign their privileges and functions would remain untouched. Since here one is not dealing with the military conquest of a foreign country, the zeal with which the head of a party — that up until not too long ago used to call itself Communist — saw fit to reassure bankers and capitalists by pointing out how well the lira and the stock exchange had received the blow is, to say the least, inappropriate. This much is certain: these politicians will end up being defeated by their very will to win at all costs. The desire to be the establishment will ruin them just as it ruined their predecessors.[6]

It is important to be able to distinguish between defeat and dishonor. The victory of the right in the 1994 political elections was a defeat for the left, which does not imply that because of this it was also a dishonor. If, as is certainly the case, this defeat also involved dishonor, that is because it marked the conclusive moment of a process of involution that had already begun many years ago. There was dishonor because the defeat did not conclude a struggle over opposite positions, but rather decided only whose turn it was to put into practice the same ideology of the spectacle, of the market, and of enterprise. One might see in this nothing other than a necessary consequence of a betrayal that had already begun in the years of Stalinism. Perhaps so. What concerns us here, however, is only the evolution that has taken place beginning with the end of the 1970s. It is since then, in fact, that the complete corruption of minds has taken that hypocritical form and that voice of reason and common sense that today goes under the name of progressivism.

In a recent book, Jean-Claude Milner has clearly identified and defined as "progressivism" the principle in whose name the following process has taken place: compromising. The revolution used to have to compromise with capital and with power, just as the church had to come to terms with the modern world. Thus, the motto that has guided the strategy of progressivism during the march toward its coming to power slowly took shape: one has to yield on everything, one has to reconcile everything with its opposite, intelligence with television and advertisement, the working class with capital, freedom of speech with the state of the spectacle, the environment with industrial development, science with opinion, democracy with the electoral machine, bad conscience and abjuration with memory and loyalty.

Today one can see what such a strategy has led to. The left has actively collaborated in setting up in every field the instruments and terms of agreement that the right, once in power, will just need to apply and develop so as to achieve its own goals without difficulty.

It was exactly in the same way that the working class was spiritually and physically disarmed by German social democracy before being handed over to Nazism. And while the citizens of goodwill are being called on to keep watch and to wait for phantasmatic frontal attacks, the right has already crossed the lines through the breach that the left itself had opened up.

Classical politics used to distinguish clearly between *zoē* and *bios*, between natural life and political life, between human beings as simply living beings, whose place was in the home, and human beings as political subjects, whose place was in the polis. Well, we no longer have any idea of any of this. We can no longer distinguish between *zoē* and *bios*, between our biological life as living beings and our political existence, between what is incommunicable and speechless and what is speakable and communicable. As Foucault once wrote, we are animals in whose politics our very life as living beings is at stake. Living in the state of exception that has now become the rule has meant also this: our private biological body has become indistinguishable from our body politic, experiences that once used to be called political suddenly were confined to our biological body, and private experiences present themselves all of a sudden outside us as body politic. We have had to grow used to thinking and writing in such a confusion of bodies and places, of outside and inside, of what is speechless and what has words with which to speak, of what is enslaved and what is free, of what is need and what is desire. This has meant—why not admit it?—experiencing absolute impotence, bumping against solitude and speechlessness over and over again precisely there where we were expecting company and words. We have endured such an impotence as best we could while being surrounded on every side by the din of the media, which were defining the new planetary political space in which exception had become the rule. But it is by starting from this uncertain terrain and from this opaque zone of indistinction that today we must once again find the path of another politics, of another body, of another word. I would not feel up to forgoing this indistinction of public and private, of biological body and body politic, of *zoē* and *bios*, for any reason whatsoever. It is here that I must find my space once again—here or nowhere else. Only a politics that starts from such an awareness can interest me.

I remember that in 1966, while attending the seminar on Heraclitus at Le Thor, I asked Heidegger whether he had read Kafka. He answered that, of the little he had read, it was above all the short story "Der Bau" (The burrow) that had made an impression on him. The nameless animal that is the protagonist of the story—mole, fox, or human being—is obsessively engaged in building an inexpugnable burrow that instead slowly reveals itself to be a trap with no way out. But isn't this precisely what has happened in the political space of Western nation-states? The homes — the "fatherlands" — that these states endeavored to build revealed themselves in the end to be only lethal traps for the very "peoples" that were supposed to inhabit them.

Beginning with the end of World War I, in fact, it is evident that the European nation-states no longer have any assignable historical tasks. To see the great totalitarian experiments of the twentieth century only as the continuation and execution of the last tasks of nineteenth-century nation-states — that is, of nationalism and imperialism — is to misunderstand completely the nature of such experiments. There are other, more extreme stakes here, because it was a question of turning into and undertaking as a task the factitious existence of peoples pure and simple — that is, in the last instance, their naked life. In this sense, the totalitarianisms of our century truly constitute the other side of the Hegelo-Kojèvian idea of an end of history: humankind has by now reached its historical telos and all that is left to accomplish is to depoliticize human societies either by unfolding unconditionally the reign of *oikonomia* or by undertaking biological life itself as supreme political task. But as soon as the home becomes the political paradigm — as is the case in both instances — then the proper, what is most one's own, and the innermost factitiousness of existence run the risk of turning into a fatal trap. And this is the trap we live in today.

In a crucial passage of the *Nicomachean Ethics*, Aristotle wonders whether there is such a thing as an *ergon*, a being-in-the-act, a being-operative, and a work proper to man, or whether man as such might perhaps be essentially *argōs*, that is, without a work, workless [*inoperoso*]:

> For just as the goodness and performance of a flute player, a sculptor, or any kind of expert, and generally of anyone who fulfills some function or performs some action, are thought to reside in his proper function [*ergon*], so the goodness and performance of man would seem to reside in whatever is his proper function. Is it then possible that while a carpenter and a shoemaker have their own proper function and spheres of action, man as man has none, but was left by nature a good-for-nothing without a function [*argōs*]?[7]

Politics is that which corresponds to the essential inoperability [*inoperosità*] of humankind, to the radical being-without-work of human communities. There is politics because human beings are *argōs*-beings that cannot be defined by any proper operation — that is, beings of pure potentiality that no identity or vocation can possibly exhaust. (This is the true political meaning of Averroism, which links the political vocation of man to the potentiality of the intellect.) Over and beyond the planetary rule of the *oikonomia* of naked life, the issue of the coming politics is the way in which this *argīa*, this essential potentiality and inoperability, might be undertaken without becoming a historical task, or, in other words, the way in which politics might be nothing other than the exposition of humankind's absence of work as well as the exposition of humankind's creative semi-indifference to any task, and might only in this sense remain integrally assigned to happiness.

E. M. Forster relates how during one of his conversations with C. P. Cavafy in Alexandria, the poet told him: "You English cannot understand us: we Greeks went bankrupt a long time ago." I believe that one of the few things that can be declared with certainty is that, since then, all the peoples of Europe (and, perhaps, all the peoples of the Earth) have gone bankrupt. *We live after the failure of peoples*, just as Apollinaire would say of himself: "I lived in the time when the kings would die." Every people has had its particular way of going bankrupt, and certainly it does make a difference that for the Germans it meant Hitler and Auschwitz, for the Spanish it meant a civil war, for the French it meant Vichy, for other people, instead, it meant the quiet and atrocious 1950s, and for the Serbs it meant the rapes of Omarska; in the end, what is crucial for us is only the new task that such a failure has bequeathed us. Perhaps it is not even accurate to define it as a task, because there is no longer a people to undertake it. As the Alexandrian poet might say today with a smile: "Now, at last, we can understand one another, because you too have gone bankrupt."

(1995)

Translators' Notes

Preface

1. The term *naked life* translates the Italian *nuda vita*. This term appears also in the subtitle of Giorgio Agamben's *Homo Sacer: il potere sovrano e la nuda vita*, as well as throughout that work. We have decided not to follow Daniel Heller-Roazen's translation of *nuda vita* as "bare life" — see *Homo Sacer: Sovereign Power and Bare Life* (Stanford, Calif.: Stanford University Press, 1998), and Daniel Heller-Roazen — and to retain the earlier translation of *nuda vita* as "naked life" to be found in Cesare Casarino's translation of Agamben's essay "Forma-di-vita" (see "Form-of-Life" in the collection edited by Paolo Virno and Michael Hardt, *A Potential Politics: Radical Thought in Italy* [Minneapolis: University of Minnesota Press, 1996], pp. 151–56).

Form-of-Life

1. The English term *power* corresponds to two distinct terms in Italian, *potenza* and *potere* (which roughly correspond to the French *puissance* and *pouvoir*, the German *Macht* and *Vermögen*, and the Latin *potentia* and *potestas*, respectively). *Potenza* can often resonate with implications of potentiality as well as with decentralized or mass conceptions of force and strength. *Potere*, on the other hand, refers to the might or authority of an already structured and centralized capacity, often an institutional apparatus such as the state.

2. Marsilius of Padua, *The Defensor of Peace*, trans. Alan Gewirth (New York: Harper and Row, 1956), p. 15; translation modified.

3. See Yan Thomas, "*Vita necisque potestas*: Le père, la cité, la mort," in *Du châtiment dans la cité: Supplices corporels et peine de mort dans le monde antique* (Rome: L'École française de Rome, 1984).

4. Walter Benjamin, "Theses on the Philosophy of History," in *Illuminations*, trans. Harry Zohn (New York: Schocken Books, 1989), p. 257. In the Italian translation of Benjamin's passage, "state of emergency" is translated as "state of exception," which is the phrase Agamben uses in the preceding section of this essay and which will be a crucial refrain in several of the other essays included in this volume.

5. "Experimental life" is in English in the original.

6. See, for example, Peter Medawar and Jean Medawar, *Aristotle to Zoos* (Oxford: Oxford University Press, 1983), pp. 66–67.

7. The terminology in the original is the same as that used for bank transactions (and thus "naked life" becomes here the cash reserve contained in accounts such as the "forms of life").

8. Aristotle, *On the Soul*, in *The Complete Works of Aristotle*, vol. 1, ed. Jonathan Barnes (Princeton, N.J.: Princeton University Press, 1984), pp. 682–83.

9. Dante Alighieri, *On World-Government*, trans. Herbert W. Schneider (Indianapolis: Liberal Arts, 1957), pp. 6–7; translation modified.

10. In English in the original. This term is taken from a single reference by Marx, in which he uses the English term. See Karl Marx, *Grundrisse: Foundations of the Critique of Political Economy*, trans. Martin Nicolaus (New York: Random House, 1973), p. 706.

Beyond Human Rights

1. Hannah Arendt, "We Refugees," *Menorah Journal*, no. 1 (1943): 77.

2. Hannah Arendt, *Imperialism*, Part II of *The Origins of Totalitarianism* (New York: Harcourt, Brace, 1951), pp. 266–98.

3. Ibid., pp. 290–95.

4. Tomas Hammar, *Democracy and the Nation State: Aliens, Denizens, and Citizens in a World of International Migration* (Brookfield, Vt.: Gower, 1990).

What Is a People?

1. Hannah Arendt, *On Revolution* (New York: Viking Press, 1963), p. 70.

Notes on Gesture

1. Gilles de la Tourette, *Études cliniques et physiologiques sur la marche* (Paris: Bureaux de progrès, 1886).

2. Jean-Martin Charcot, *Charcot, the Clinician: The Tuesday Lessons* (New York: Raven Press, 1987).

3. See Gilles Deleuze, *Cinema 1: The Movement-Image*, trans. Hugh Tomlinson and Barbara Habberjam (Minneapolis: University of Minnesota Press, 1986).

4. Varro, *On the Latin Language*, trans. Roland G. Kent (Cambridge: Harvard University Press, 1977), p. 245.

5. Aristotle, *Nicomachean Ethics*, trans. Martin Ostwald (Indianapolis: Bobbs-Merrill Educational Publishing, 1983), p. 153.

Languages and Peoples

1. François De Vaux de Foletier, *Les Tsiganes dans l'ancienne France*; cited in Alice Becker-Ho, *Les princes du jargon: Un facteur négligé aux origines de l'argot des classes dangereuses; Édition augmentée* (Paris: Gallimard, 1993), pp. 22–23.

2. The reference is to Alice Becker-Ho, *Les princes du jargon: Un facteur négligé aux origines de l'argot des classes dangereuses* (Paris: Gérard Lebovici, 1990).

3. Becker-Ho, *Les princes du jargon; Édition augmentée*, p. 51.

4. Ibid., p. 50.

5. Gershom Scholem, "Une lettre inédite de Gershom Scholem à Franz Rosenzweig: À propos de notre langue. Une confession," trans. from German into French by Stefan Moses, *Archives des Sciences Sociales des Religions et Archives de Sociologie des Religions* 60:1 (Paris, 1985): 83–84.

Marginal Notes on *Commentaries on the Society of the Spectacle*

1. Karl von Clausewitz, cited in Guy Debord, *Préface à la quatrième édition italienne de "La Société du Spectacle"* (Paris: Éditions Champ Libre, 1979), pp. 15–16.

2. We have translated this passage from the Italian as we could not find the original reference.

3. Karl Marx, *Capital*, vol. 1, trans. Ben Fowkes (New York: Vintage Books, 1977), p. 165.

4. Louis Althusser, "Preface to *Capital* Volume One," in *Lenin and Philosophy*, trans. Ben Brewster (New York: Monthly Review Press, 1971), p. 95; but see the whole essay, and especially pp. 81 and 88.

5. Karl Kraus, "In These Great Times," in *In These Great Times*, trans. Harry Zohn (Montreal: Engendra Press, 1976), p. 70.

6. Friedrich Nietzsche, *The Gay Science*, trans. Walter Kaufmann (New York: Vintage Books, 1974), pp. 273–74.

The Face

1. Franz Rosenzweig, *The Star of Redemption*, trans. William W. Hallo (New York:

Holt, Rinehart and Winston, 1970), pp. 422–23.

Sovereign Police

1. Walter Benjamin, "Critique of Violence," in *Reflections*, trans. Edmund Jephcott (New York: Schocken Books, 1986), p. 287.

Notes on Politics

1. Walter Benjamin, "Theologico-Political Fragment," in *Reflections*, trans. Edmund Jephcott (New York: Schocken Books, 1986), p. 312.

In This Exile (Italian Diary, 1992–94)

1. Ayrtan Senna — Brazilian race-car driver and charismatic public icon — died in Italy during the San Marino Grand Prix at the age of thirty-four. His death was a highly publicized media event.

2. Bettino Craxi was head of the PSI (Italian Socialist Party) from 1976 to 1987, as well as Italian prime minister from 1983 to 1986. In the early 1990s, he was at the center of the *Tangentopoli* scandal, was accused of corruption, and fled Italy for Tunisia, where he died in early 2000.

3. Giovanni Botero, *The Reason of State*, trans. P. J. and D. P. Waley (New Haven: Yale University Press, 1956), p. 3.

4. Here Agamben is referring to the controversial phenomenon of *pentitismo*, which ignited public opinion in Italy throughout the 1990s. *Pentiti* — "turncoats," or, literally, "the ones who have repented" — are former members of organized crime or of left-wing or right-wing political organizations who decide to disavow their beliefs publicly and to name other members of their organizations during police investigations or trials in exchange for immunity or reduced prison terms.

5. Karl Marx, *The Letters of Karl Marx*, trans. Saul K. Padover (Englewood Cliffs, N.J.: Prentice Hall, 1979), p. 24.

6. The term *establishment* is in English in the original.

7. Aristotle, *Nicomachean Ethics*, book 1, trans. Martin Ostwald (Indianapolis: Liberal Arts Press, 1962), p. 16.

Index

Giorgio Agamben is professor of philosophy at the University of Verona. Many of his works have been translated into English, including *Language and Death* (1991), *Stanzas* (1992), and *The Coming Community* (1993), all published by the University of Minnesota Press.

Vincenzo Binetti is assistant professor of Romance languages and literatures at the University of Michigan.

Cesare Casarino is assistant professor of cultural studies and comparative literature at the University of Minnesota.